FOR LOVE ALONE

FOR
LOVE ALONE

Reflections on priestly celibacy

ST PAULS

Original title: *Solo per amore. Riflessioni sul celibato sacerdotale.* (03850

© 1993 Edizioni Paoline s.r.l., Cinisello Balsamo, Italy.

The reflections by Ignace de la Potterie, Max Turian, Crescenzio Sepe, Jerome Lejeune, Wanda Plotawska, Julianus Voronovsky, Damaskinos Papandreou, Maria Adelaide Raschini, Divo Barsotti, José Saraiva Martins were translated from the Italian by Alan Neame.

Cover design: EP srl

ST PAULS
Middlegreen, Slough SL3 6BT, United Kingdom
Moyglare Road, Maynooth, Co. Kildare, Ireland

English translation © ST PAULS 1993

ISBN 085439 449 4

Produced in the EEC

Printed by The Guernsey Press Co. Ltd, Guernsey, C.I.

ST PAULS is an activity of the priests and brothers of the Society of St Paul who proclaim the Gospel through the media of social communication

Contents

Preface (*José T. Sánchez*)   7

The biblical foundation of priestly celibacy
(*Ignace de la Potterie*)   13

Priestly celibacy in patristic and in the history
of the Church (*Roman Cholij*)   31

The theological basis for priestly celibacy
(*Max Thurian*)   53

The relevance of priestly celibacy today
(*Crescenzio Sepe*)   66

Coeli Beatus: Observations of a biologist
(*Jerôme Lejeune*)   83

Priestly celibacy in the light of medicine and
psychology (*Wanda Poltawska*)   89

Priestly celibacy and problems of inculturation
(*Polycarp Pengo*)   103

The Oriental Rite Churches and priestly celibacy
(*Julianus Voronovsky*)   112

The Orthodox Churches and priestly celibacy
(*Damaskinos Papandreou*)   119

The Anglican Communion and priestly celibacy
(*Davis Michael Hope*)   123

Purity and the priesthood in the Hebrew Scriptures
and Rabbinic tradition (*Jacob Neusner*)   129

An Oriental Church returns to unity
choosing priestly celibacy
(*Benedict Varghese Gregorios Thangalathil*)   137

Celibacy: Fidelity to one's priestly identity
(*Dominic Tang Yee-ming*) 147

Point of view of a Zen monk from Japan
(*Soko Morinaga*) 154

Priestly celibacy: Misogyny of the Catholic Church?
(*Maria Adelaide Raschini*) 160

The spirituality of priestly celibacy
(*Divo Barsotti*) 179

Training for priestly celibacy
(*José Saraiva Martins*) 186

Priestly celibacy: Sign of the charity of Christ
(*Mother Teresa of Calcutta*) 210

Preface

José T. Sánchez

Prefect of the Congregation for the Clergy

The Council Fathers of Vatican II, profoundly convinced of the important role of the clergy in the renewal of the Church, said: "This sacred Council has already on several occasions drawn the attention of the world to the excellence of the order of priests in the Church. Since, however, a most important and increasingly difficult role is being assigned to this order in the renewal of Christ's Church, it has been thought that it would be extremely useful to treat the priesthood at greater length and depth" (PO 1). In fact they declared: "The Council is fully aware that the desired renewal of the whole Church depends in great part upon a priestly ministry animated by the spirit of Christ" (OT 1).

Aware or not of this firm conviction of the Council Fathers of Vatican II, the communications media in a significant part of the world have focused public attention on the Catholic priesthood, with particular emphasis on its declining numbers and have felt a gap between the expectation of the people and the actual performance of the members of the clergy. They highlight the increasing number of parishes without priests as well as the other unattended fields of the apostolate because of lack of priests. Similarly, they point to the reduced number of students for the priesthood. Alongside this failure in number, the media lament the absence of pastoral leadership that people were accustomed to finding in the clergy. They miss that dedicated service and pastoral leadership that projected both the universal and local dimension of the one Church all over the world and inspired the faithful to be proud to belong to the Church and to participate in its mission.

For both ills the media blame *celibacy*. Celibacy is

claimed to be the cause both of defections in the ranks of the clergy, and of closing the door to possible aspirants to the priesthood.

A close examination, however, of the situation of the clergy today does not justify either the premises or the conclusions. While it is conceded that in some parts of the Church, particularly in Western Europe and in North America, which used to have abundant clergy to enable them to supply the personnel needs of the missionary Church, a significant drop in the number of priests has indeed taken place until recently. This drop was not due to defections that could be attributed solely to celibacy. Celibacy was just one of the varied causes that led some priests to leave the priesthood. These are, moreover, insignificantly few compared to those who remain faithful to the end.

A cause of the diminishing number of priests in the 'active ministry', is certainly, at least partially, the widespread practice of priests being able to retire from parochial responsibility when reaching a certain age. The priest, however, by reason of his vocation, even if he puts aside a specific assignment, continues in ministry until death because the idea of 'retirement' in the commonly understood sense of the word is fundamentally foreign to the concept of 'priesthood': the pastoral office is not given 'ad tempus', but becomes part of the person's 'identity' and not merely of his 'actions'. Priesthood is an eloquent demonstration of everything about the person; one does not refer to a 'functionary', so much as to 'another Christ'.

It is also conceded that in some areas, until recently, there had been few priestly ordinations. Indeed apprehension was felt that there would not be enough young priests to replace those who had died, were sick, had left the ministry and those who had retired. Lately however, a slow but steady increase in priestly ordinations and vocations has emerged. Moreover, in Africa, Asia, Central and South America a steady increase in priestly vocations and ordinations has been maintained. Presently, a boom in priestly vocation is taking place in these Churches. If celibacy were the cause of a drop in the priestly vocation it should apply to the whole Latin Church. The different situations as far as priestly vocations are concerned, abundance in some and scarcity in others, must find an explanation in other factors that have different prevalence in diverse areas and not in celibacy which is common to all areas.

The Catholic priesthood must be considered in its supernatural perspective

The priestly vocation and ministry must be seen and considered in their proper perspective, namely, that they are a divine gift. The priest is called and chosen by God for a specific purpose in God's plan in the salvation of humanity. To consider and judge his vocation on purely human terms would inevitably lead to fallacious conclusions. St Peter himself experienced this when he confessed that Christ was the Son of the living God and thereby earned that unforgettable affirmation from the Lord: "Blessed are you Simon, son of Jonah. No mere man has revealed this to you, but my heavenly Father" (Mt 16:17). And yet, just a little while later when following merely his human agenda Peter remonstrated against the Lord's announcement of his coming passion, death and resurrection, he received from the Lord a very severe rebuke: "Get out of my sight, you Satan," Jesus said to Peter, "you are not judging by God's standards but by man's" (Mt 16:23).

The Catholic priesthood is God's precious gift to redeemed humanity

The ministerial priesthood is a manifestation of God's infinite love for humanity while the priestly ministry as accepted by humanity is hamanity's answer to God's love.

9

"Yes, God so loved the world, that he gave his only Son, that whoever believes in him may not die but may have eternal life" (Jn 3:16). Indeed when the people who in the utterly gratuitous design of God's wisdom and goodness were raised to share in God's own divine life failed in Adam, he did not abandon them; he offered them means of salvation (LG 2). "God did not send the Son into the world to condemn the world, but that the world might be saved through him" (Jn 3:17). Accordingly, Christ came and laid down his life for us thereby proving how great was his love for us because he himself said: "There is no greater love than this: to lay down one's life for one's friends" (Jn 15:13).

To perpetuate this dispensation of the grace of redemption to all people of all times and places, Christ makes his whole Mystical Body share in the anointing of the Spirit making of his people a holy and kingly priesthood (1 Pet 2:5, 9). At the same time he chose the apostles and their successors "to hold in the community of the faithful the sacred order, that of offering sacrifice and forgiving sins, and exercise of priestly office publicly on behalf of men in the name of Christ" (PO 2). "Priests, through holy orders, are signed with a special character and so are configured to Christ the priest in such a way that they are able to act in the person of Christ the Head" (PO 2).

Harmony between priesthood and celibacy

Raised to such a sublime dignity and conscious of the gratuitousness of this gift of God, priests feel that they can do nothing less than make Christ their direct model and sublime ideal as part of their total consecration to God and the service of his people. Christ, in doing his Father's will, "emptied himself and took the form of a slave... and humbled himself, obediently accepting even death, death on a cross" (Phil 2:7-8). Moreover, Christ remained throughout his earthly life in a state of virginity which signified a complete consecration to the service of God and God's people. This profound connection between virginity and the priesthood of Christ is reflected in those who are called and chosen to participate in the dignity and mission of the Eternal Priest, and this participation will become more perfect when it is free from the bonds of flesh and blood. This is the reason why the Latin Church has maintained *celibacy* as a vital element of the priest's total consecration to God and unhampered service to God's people.

Celibacy is not demanded of the priesthood by its nature; but there are many ways in which celibacy is in harmony with the priesthood

The whole mission of the priest is dedicated to the service of the new humanity redeemed by Christ as a participation in the eternal priesthood of Christ. By preserving celibacy for the kingdom of heaven, priests are consecrated in a new and excellent way to Christ; they more readily cling to him with an undivided heart (1 Cor 7:32-34) and dedicate themselves more freely in him and through him to the service of God and thereby of his people. They are less encumbered in their service of his kingdom and of the task of heavenly regeneration. In this way they become better fitted for a broader acceptance of the fatherhood in Christ (cf PO 16).

This book which brings together in one volume the convictions and experiences of men and women of varied backgrounds: intellectual, social, ecclesial (Latin or Oriental and non-Catholic) and non-Christian, young and old, is intended to help all, particularly the members of the clergy insofar as they are called to the priesthood, to realize that while celibacy is not required by the nature of the priesthood, it is nevertheless a natural complement to the priestly consecration and a real desire to reciprocate the infinite love of Christ with total human love. Would that this book could help us to realize that we can better comprehend the value and beauty of priestly celibacy only when it is related to the priesthood of Christ and with the style of his life. This is crucial to a deeper understanding of priestly celibacy. The Lord himself affirmed that not all can understand celibacy for the kingdom of God, but only those to whom God gives the grace to understand. In fact, speaking of the priesthood we are told that "one does not take this honour on his own initiative, but only when called by God as Aaron was" (Heb 5:4).

The biblical foundation of priestly celibacy

Ignace de la Potterie

Biblical scholar

For several centuries there has been much debate as to whether the obligation of celibacy for clerics in major orders (or at least that of living in continence for those who are married) is of biblical origin or whether it is based merely on ecclesiastical tradition dating back to the fourth century, since from then on, without question, legislation exists on the subject. The first of these two possible answers has recently been presented once again, this time with an extraordinary wealth of material, by C. Cochini in *Origines apostoliques du célibat sacerdotal*.[1] Clearly set forth in the title, the author's position is apparently that celibacy can be and should be upheld, given that account is taken (more perhaps than in the past) of the growth of ancient tradition, a point on which A.M. Stickler also insists in his preface,[2] and H. Crouzel in a review.[3] In other words, it could be said that the *obligation* of continence (or of celibacy) became canon law only in the fourth century but that, before that, from apostolic times, the ideal of living in continence (or in celibacy) was already held up to the ministers of the Church, and that this ideal was indeed deeply felt and lived as a requirement by quite a number (Tertullian and Origen, for instance) but was not yet imposed on all clerics in major orders. It was a vital principle, a seed, clearly present from apostolic times but which gradually then developed until the ecclesiastical legislation of the fourth century.[4]

The new *Catechism of the Catholic Church* (n. 1579) seems to take the same line. Out of prudence, however, it omits to mention the canon law on celibacy, which none-theless forms part of Church law today (*CIC* 277 par. 1), and merely sets out the biblical reasons for celibacy. Yet even here it no longer refers (as often in the past) to the Old Testament, and only quotes two passages from the New: the one in Matthew 19:22, *about celibacy*: "for the sake of the kingdom of heaven"; and then the Pauline text of 1 Corinthians 7:32-35, where the Apostle speaks of those who are called to consecrate themselves with undivided heart to the Lord and "his affairs"; and adds by way of conclusion that "embraced with a joyful heart, it (the celibate life) radiantly proclaims the kingdom of God". Here of course one might quote other New Testament passages to which, for instance, Paul VI referred in his encyclical *Sacerdotalis coelibatus* (nn. 17-35), to indicate the reasons for sacred celibacy (its Christological, ecclesiological and eschatological significance). But the problem is that these various texts describe, as a typically Christian ideal, the theological and spiritual value of celibacy *in genere*. This ideal, however, is equally valid for the religious and for people living consecrated lives in the world; they do not show any particular connection with the *ministries* of the Church.

The precise question that arises, therefore, is this: do texts exist in Holy Writ which point to a specific connection between celibacy and priesthood? It would seem so. But if this is the case, more importance will have to be attached to certain New Testament passages which (oddly) have not received much attention in the recent debates. These are the texts in which the Pauline norm (much contested, to be sure) of '*unius uxoris vir*'[5] is set out, for analysis of which C. Cochini has also now adduced new material. Enunciated several times in the Pastoral Letters, this principle is uniquely important in our case for two reasons. The first is, as has been convincingly shown by Stickler[6] as well as by Cochini,[7] that the stipulation was one of the main formulae on which the ancient tradition was based for claiming an actual apostolic origin for the law of *priestly celibacy*. This was, of course, an immense paradox: how can one base the *celibacy* of priests on the evidence of texts which talk about *married* ministers? Such reasoning can only make sense if there is a middle term between the two extremes (marriage of ministers and celibacy): it is that of *continence,* to which, in fact, *married* ministers were bound. It was probably because this mediating value of *continence* was overlooked, that in recent times the formula *unius uxoris vir* dropped out of discussions on *celibacy*. It is therefore timely today to re-examine carefully the traditional argument.

The other reason why these texts are especially important from the strictly biblical point of view lies in the fact that they are the only passages in the New Testament where an identical norm is laid down for the three groups of *ordained ministers,* and only for them. For, according to the Pastoral Letters, the bishop ought to be *unius uxoris vir* (1 Tim 3:2), so ought the priest (Tit 1:6) and so ought the deacon (1 Tim 3:12), whereas that formula (a technical one, it would seem) is never used for other Christians. So here we have a special requirement for the exercise of the *ministerial priesthood* as such. Further, it should also be observed that the complementary formula *unius viri uxor* (1 Tim 5:9) is only used of widows at least 60 years old. That is to say, it does not apply to any Christian woman only but to elderly women who exercise a *ministry* in the community (comparable, one imagines, with that of deaconesses in ancient times). The stereotyped character of this formula in the Pastoral Letters makes one suspect it must have already been rooted in a long biblical tradition.[8]

So what does it mean that the *minister* of the Church should be "the husband of one wife"? In the following pages we shall first try to show that the formula *unius uxoris vir*, up to the fourth century, was understood, as Stickler so well puts it, "in the sense of a biblical argument in favour of *celibacy* of *apostolic* inspiration: for the Pauline norm was interpreted in the sense of a guarantee assuring effective observance of *continence* by *ministers* who were

15

already married before they were ordained."[9] In the second part, we shall take a step forward: we shall propose a deeper theological interpretation of the Pauline stipulation itself, to show that, already in New Testament times it actually does propose the model for the ministerial priesthood of a marital relationship between Christ the bridegroom and the Church his bride, on the basis of the mystical view of marriage which St Paul frequently mentions in his letters (cf 2 Cor 11:2; Eph 5:22-32).[10] From this, it will become abundantly clear that, for married ministers, their ordination implied an invitation to live in continence thereafter.

The stipulation *unius uxoris vir*: an argument in ancient tradition for the apostolic origin of celibacy/continence

a. Ecclesiastical legislation from the fourth century onwards

Scholars generally agree that the obligation of celibacy, or at least of continence, became canon law from the fourth century onwards. Here certain incontrovertible texts are quoted repeatedly: three pontifical decretals around AD 385 (*Decreta* and *Cum in unum* of Pope Siricius and *Dominus inter* of Siricius or Damasus) and a canon of the Council of Carthage of AD 390.[11]

However, it is important to observe that the legislators of the fourth and fifth centuries affirmed that this canonical enactment was based on an apostolic tradition. The Council of Carthage, for instance, saidthat it was fitting that those who were at the service of the divine sacraments be perfectly continent (*continentes esse in omnibus*): "so that what the apostles taught and antiquity itself maintained, we too may observe".[12] The decree on the obligation of *continence* was then passed unanimously: "It is pleasing to all that bishop, priest and deacon, the guardians of purity, abstain from marital relations with their wives (*ab uxoribus se abstineant*) so that the perfect purity may be safeguarded of those who serve the altar."

The Pauline *unius uxoris vir* is not explicitly quoted here but reference to this stipulation is implicit since, as in the Pastoral Letters, the bishop, priest and deacon each are mentioned. Besides, 1 Timothy 3:2 is quoted explicitly in an earlier text, the decretal *Cum in unum* of Siricius himself, who presented the norms of the Council of Rome of AD 386. Here the Pope first formulated an objection that the expression *unius uxoris vir* of 1 Timothy 3:2, some said, specifically guaranteed the bishop the right *to use* marriage after sacred ordination. Siricius answered by giving the stipulation's correct interpretation: "He (Paul) was not speaking of a man who might persist in the desire to beget children (*non permanentem in desiderio generandi dixit*); he was speaking about continence which they had to observe in future (*propter continentiam futuram*)." This fundamental text was repeated a number of times subsequently.[13] This is Cochini's comment on it: "Monogamy (that is to say, the law of *unius uxoris vir*) is a condition for receiving Order, since faithfulness (observed *up till then*) to one woman is warranty for supposing that the candidate will be capable (*in the future*) of practising the perfect continence to be asked of him after ordination."[14] And the author goes on: "This exegesis of St Paul's prescriptions to Timothy and Titus is an essential link by which the bishops of the Synod of Rome (AD 386) and Pope Siricius are cited in continuity with the apostolic age."

But is this exegesis, for which an apostolic tradition is claimed, properly founded? Not without reason, some scholars think it doubtful.[15] For certain questions have to be asked: is it not rather odd to discover in the *past* behaviour of the married minister (that is to say, his faithfulness to one woman, even in sexual relations) a sufficient guarantee of his *future* but *different behaviour* (that is, continence in conjugal relations with that same woman, his lawful wife)?

17

The legislators saw in the past a guarantee for the future, but at the same time they changed the tune to be played: from the (lawful) *use* of marriage to *renunciation* of it. To justify this twofold transition from past to future and from sexual relations to conjugal continence, we need an explanatory *tertium quid*: such justification is only possible if an interpretation of this same formula can be found to bring out, perhaps, some hidden and hitherto unnoted aspect. And this is what we shall try to do in the second part.

But first let us briefly investigate whether, in the history of exegesis and canonical legislation, there may not be elements that can lead us to a deeper understanding of the Pauline stipulation.

b. Theological reasons for the continence and celibacy of priests

From the patristic period until today, we find ourselves faced with two different interpretations of the Pauline formula: for some people, the norm *unius uxoris vir* prohibits *serial* polygamy; for others, only simultaneous polygamy.[16]

The first solution is undoubtedly the more traditional: the expression then means that the sacred ministers could be married men, but only married once; and if the wife had died, they must not have contracted a second marriage, nor could they marry again later. Today, too, this interpretation is the more commonly held among Catholic exegetes. According to the other solutions, however, *unius uxoris vir* means only being forbidden to live with more than one woman at the same time; it would thus simply be a recommendation to observe conjugal morality.

But neither of these two solutions is entirely satisfying. To the first, it can be objected: if the union in which the married minister was hitherto living was virtuous, why should a second marriage not be so, after the first wife's death? It is also the case that the Apostle himself on the one hand required the elderly widow who served the community to have been *unius viri uxor* (1 Tim 5:9), whereas he advised young widows to get married again (1 Tim 5:14). But the other solution raises problems too: conjugal faithfulness in married life is certainly required of all Christians. Why then is the expression *unius uxoris vir* (and analogously *unius viri uxor*) used only for those who exercise a *ministry* in the community?

We may add that the second interpretation goes no further than the simple level of general morality; applied to ministers of the Church, it has something commonplace and reductive about it. The first – the prohibition of a second marriage – is rather of a disciplinary and canonical nature, but its theological basis is not indicated. The same omission has indeed already been noted in the canonical legislation of the fourth century: Pope Siricius and many others after him interpreted the Pauline stipulation as the *obligation* to continence for the married clergy. They did, it is true, give their reason: the purity required of those approaching the altar. But it has to be recognized that this is not in fact what is being talked about in the text of the Pastoral Letters.

At the end of Stickler's historical investigation, he too recognized that, in this whole problem of priestly celibacy, there had been too much concentration on the juridical aspect.[17] Throughout that lengthy history there had been a lack of theological reflection on the deeper significance of the ministerial priesthood, on the reason for its celibacy and on its spiritual value. This is particularly true of the canonical use of the norm *unius uxoris vir* from the fourth century onwards. So we shall have to search the patristic and canonical tradition itself to see if any theological reasons are given for basing the disciplinary obligation of clerical continence on the Pauline stipulation.

Three pieces of evidence are significant here. The first is provided by Tertullian at the beginning of the third century. He reminds the clergy that monogamy is not only an ecclesiastical discipline but also a precept of the Apostle.[18] It thus dates back to apostolic times. Furthermore, he insists on the fact that, in the Church, not a few believers are not married, that they live in *continence* and that some of them belong to 'ecclesiastical orders'.[19] Now, the men and women who live like this, Tertullian goes on, "have preferred to marry God" (*Deo nubere maluerunt*);[20] and speaking about virgins, he says that they are "brides of Christ".[21]

But what is the connection between *monogamous* marriage on the one hand and *continence* on the other? Tertullian does not say, but here invokes the example set by Christ who, according to the flesh, was not married and lived in celibacy (he was not, therefore, "a husband of one wife"); yet, in the spirit, "he had one bride the Church" (*unam habens ecclesiam sponsam*).[22] This doctrine of Christ's spiritual marriage to the Church, here inspired by the Pauline text of Ephesians 5:25-32, was common in early Christianity; Tertullian saw this spiritual marriage as one of the main theological bases for the law of monogamous marriage: "because Christ is *one* and his Church is *one*" (*unus enim Christus et una eius ecclesia*).[23] But it does not follow from this that Tertullian had already made the connection between this doctrine and the formulae *unius uxoris vir* or *unius viri uxor* of the Pastoral Letters, where monogamous marriage is explicitly referred to; this connection between the two themes is what we shall be trying to establish further on.

Besides, in the last text quoted, Tertullian's reasoning was not soundly based: the problem dealt with in Ephesians 5:25-32 was not monogamous marriage but, in principle, the relationship of every Christian marriage with the *covenant*. Here Paul is speaking of *all* married members of the Church. When, referring to Genesis 2:24, the Apostle says that husband and wife "will be one flesh" (v. 31), he is justifying the use of marriage for them.[24] The formula *unius uxoris vir* of the Pastoral Letters, however, is not used for all married men but only for *ministers* of the Church (this fact has been too little noted); yet subsequently it came to be regarded as the biblical basis of the law of continence for clerics. This is the point that still needs to be cleared up.

With St Augustine we take a step forward. He, having taken part in the deliberationsof the African synods, was certainly aware of the ecclesiastic law governing the 'continence of clerics'.[25] But how does Augustine then explain the stipulation *unius uxoris vir* which is used by Paul for married clerics? In *De bono conjugali* (written in about AD 420), he advances a theological explanation for it, and asks himself why polygamy was accepted in the Old Testament, whereas "in our own age, the sacrament has been restricted to the union between *one man* and *one woman*; and consequently it is only lawful to ordain as a minister of the Church (*ecclesiae dispensatorem*) a man who has had one wife (*unius uxoris virum*)". And here is Augustine's answer: "As the many wives (*plures uxores*) of the ancient Fathers symbolized our future churches of all nations, subject to the one man, Christ (*uni viro subditas Christo*), so the guide of the faithful (*noster antistes*, our bishop), who is the husband of one wife (*unius uxoris vir*) signifies the union of all nations, subject to the one man, Christ (*uni viro subditam Christo*)".[26]

In this text, where we find the formula *unius uxoris vir* being applied to the *bishop*, the whole accent falls on the fact that he, 'the man', in his relations with his 'wife', symbolizes the relationship between Christ and the Church. An analogous use of the phrase 'man and wife' occurs in a passage of *De continentia*: "The Apostle invites us to observe so to speak three pairs (*copulas*): Christ and the Church, husband and wife, the spirit and the flesh".[27] The suggestion these texts offer us for interpreting the stipulation *unius uxoris vir* applied to the (married) minister of the sacrament is that he, as minister, not only represents the second pair (husband and wife) but also the first: henceforth he personifies *Christ* in his married relationship with the *Church*. Here we have the basis for the doctrine which was later to become a classic one: *Sacerdos alter Christus*. Like Christ, the priest is the Church's bridegroom.

One further word on the canonical legislation of the Middle Ages. On various occasions, in penitential books, it is said that for a married priest to go on having sexual relations with his wife after ordination would be an act of unfaithfulness to the promise made to God. It would be an *adulterium* since, the minister now being married to the Church, his relationship with his own wife "is like a violation of the marriage bond".[28] This weighty accusation against a lawfully wedded, decent man only makes sense if something is left unexpressed because it is well-known, i.e., that the sacred minister, from the moment of his ordination, now lives in another relationship, also of a matrimonial type – that which unites Christ and the Church in which he, the minister, the man (*vir*), represents Christ the bridegroom; with his own wife (*uxor*) therefore "the carnal union should from now on be a spiritual one", as St Leo the Great said.[29]

With these various historical and theological preliminaries, we have gathered enough material for us to be able to tackle the exegetical problem, that is to say, to make an accurate analysis of the actual formula *unius uxoris vir* in the Pastoral Letters.

'Unius uxoris vir': a covenantal formula

We have already seen that, of the two traditional interpretations of the stipulation, one (the more widespread) was of a disciplinary type, and the other exclusively moral. But it was virtually never explained *why* a minister of the Church should be 'the husband of one wife'. We shall now attempt to show that the reason for this norm, its deeper meaning and its implications are already present in the text itself if we succeed in analyzing it properly. First we need to clear up the problem of where this mysterious form comes from, with its undeniably fixed, technical, stereotyped nature. But let it be said forthwith: the stipulation is actually a covenantal formula.

This becomes plain when we consider the parallelism between the formula in the Pastoral Letters and the passage in 2 Corinthians 11:2, where Paul describes the Church of Corinth as a woman, as a bride, whom he has presented to Christ as a chaste virgin:

I am jealous about you with the jealousy of God, because I have betrothed you *to one man* (*uni viro*), to present you to Christ *as a pure virgin*.

The context of this passage is particularly clear if we read it with 1 Timothy 5:9. The same formula *unus vir* is used of the relations whether of the *Church* with *Christ*, or of the *widow* who has only had one *husband* and discharges a ministry in the community. In 2 Corinthians 11:2, Christ's bride is the Church itself. Let us carefully read the text over again. The jealousy of which Paul speaks is a sharing in God's jealousy over his people.[30] It is the zeal devouring the Apostle that his Christians may remain faithful to the covenant made with Christ, who is their true and only bridegroom. Another detail confirms this interpretation: the Church-bride is paradoxically presented to Christ the bridegroom as 'a pure virgin'. This is a reference to the Daughter of Sion, sometime called 'virgin Sion', 'virgin Israel' by the prophets,[31] especially when she is invited, after past infidelities, once more to be true to the covenant, to her marriage relationship with her only *Bridegroom*.

The other decisive New Testament passage is the classic text in Ephesians 5:22-23: husband and wife united in matrimony are the image of Christ and the Church. Now Christ, the bridegroom, gave himself up for the Church, so as to make her his glorious, holy and spotless bride (cf vv. 26-27). But the fact that the expression *unius uxoris vir* is not used here in the Letter to the Ephesians for all married Christians, and is reserved in the Pastoral Letters for the married *minister*, shows that the formula refers directly to the priestly ministry and the Christ-Church relationship: the minister must be like Christ the bridegroom.

We can also point out another important consequence of the connection between the *unius uxoris vir* (or *unius viri uxor*) of the Pastoral Letters and the passage in 2 Corinthians 11:2. It is that the Church-bride is called a 'pure virgin'. Marital love between Christ the bridegroom and his bride the Church is ever a *virginal* love.

For the Church of Corinth (where obviously the great majority of Christians were married), it was an immediate question of what St Augustine calls *virginitas fidei, virginitas cordis*, unblemished faith,[32] well described also by St Leo the Great: "*Discat Sponsa Verbi non alium virum nosse quam Christum*".[33] But for the married ministers of whom the Pastoral Letters speak, it is the norm that – in that mystical view of their ministry – the radical call to *virginitas cordis* should also be lived by them as a call to *virginitas carnis* as regards their wives, that is to say, as a call to continence, as becomes clear in Tradition, at least from the fourth century onwards. So we are now no longer dealing with an external, ecclesiastical prescription but rather with an inner perception of the fact that ordination makes the priestly minister a representation of Christ the bridegroom in relation to the Church, bride and virgin, and hence he cannot live with another wife.

The decisive relationship between the *unius uxoris vir* of the Pastoral Letters and the 'pure virgin' of 2 Corinthians 11:2 has also been well brought out by E. Tauzin: men who are consecrated to God, he says, "should represent Christ; now, he is only the bridegroom of one bride, the Church: '*Virginem castam exhibere Christo*'".[34] And he then applies this principle to the parable in Matthew 25:1-13, where the ten 'virgins', who are (in the plural) the brides of Christ, in fact present this *one* bride: "Outwardly there is multiplicity; inwardly, unity. Isn't virginity perhaps the best outward image of an inner unity?"

This sacramental and spiritual argument of the *unius uxoris vir*, based on the theology of the covenant, emerges first in the Western tradition with Tertullian, then with St Augustine and St Leo the Great. We find it well summed

24

up by St Thomas in his commentary on 1 Timothy 3:2 (*Oportet ergo episcopum... esse unius uxoris virum*): "This is so, not merely to avoid incontinence, but to represent the sacrament, since the Church's bridegroom is Christ and the Church is *one: Una est columba mea* (Song of Songs 6:9).[35] But St Thomas does not as yet make the connection with the text in 2 Corinthians 11:2, which speaks of the bride-virgin; and therefore he does not add that the representational role of the monogamous priesthood also entails the call to *continence* for the married minister, and consequently, for the unmarried ones, the call to *celibacy*.

Conclusion

In order to grasp the way in which we have tried to show the biblical basis of priestly celibacy, it is important to distinguish between celibacy and continence. In the ancient Church, many priests were married. This explains why, in speaking of the ministers of the Church, the formula *unius uxoris vir* came to be used. It also explains the great interest the Fathers had in monogamous marriage (cf for instance Tertullian: *De monogamia*). But it becomes clearer still in the Tradition that for a minister of the Church, united once in matrimony with a woman, acceptance of the ministry brought with it the consequence that he had to live in continence thereafter.

In later times, the separation was introduced between priesthood and marriage. And so the formula *unius uxoris vir*, in its literal and material sense, is no longer of immediate application to the priests of today, since they are not married. Yet paradoxically, precisely in this lies the interest of the formula. We set out from the fact that in the apostolic Church it was only used for clerics; and so it took on, besides the immediate sense of conjugal relations, a further, mystical sense, a direct connection with the spiritual marriage between Christ and the Church. St Paul was already hinting at this. For him, *unius uxoris vir* was a covenantal formula: it introduced the married minister into the marriage relationship between Christ and the Church; for Paul, the Church was a 'pure virgin', it was the 'bride' of Christ. But this connection between the minister and Christ, due to the sacrament of ordination, today no longer requires as human support for the symbolism a real marriage on the part of the minister; so the formula is still valid for priests of the Church, although they are not married. Hence, that which in the past was *continence* for married ministers, in our own day becomes the *celibacy* of those who are not. Yet the symbolic and spiritual meaning of the expression *unius uxoris vir* remains ever the same. Indeed, since it contains a direct reference to the covenant, that is to say, to the *marriage* relationship between Christ and the Church, it invites us to attach much greater importance today than in the past to the fact that the minister of the Church represents Christ the bridegroom to the Church his bride. In this sense, the priest must be "the husband of one wife"; but that one wife, his bride, is the Church who, like Mary, is the bride of Christ.

It is precisely thus that on various occasions John Paul II expresses himself in his post-synodal Apostolic Exhortation *Pastores dabo vobis*. By way of conclusion, we quote some of the more telling passages from it.

In n. 12, having said that, as regards the identity of the priest, his relationship with the Church must take second place to his relationship with Christ, the Pope goes on: "As a *mystery, the Church is essentially related to Jesus Christ.* She is his fullness, his body, his spouse... The priest finds the full truth of his identity in being a derivation, a specific participation in and continuation of Christ himself, the one High Priest of the new and eternal covenant; the priest is a living and transparent image of Christ the Priest. The priesthood of Christ, the expression of his absolute 'newness' in salvation history, constitutes the one source and essential model of the priesthood shared by all Christians and the priest in particular. Reference to Christ is thus the absolutely necessary key for understanding the reality of priesthood." On the basis of this very close union between the priest and Christ, the deep theological reason for celibacy is easier to grasp.

In some editions of the document, n. 22 bears the crosshead: "Witness to Christ's spousal love". Further on, it reads: "The priest is called to be the living image of Jesus Christ, the spouse of the Church." The Pope then quotes a proposition of the Synod: "Inasmuch as he represents Christ, the Head, Shepherd and Spouse of the Church, the priest is placed not only in the Church but also in the forefront of the Church."

In n. 29, in the very paragraph where the Holy Father speaks of virginity and celibacy, he cites in full the Synod's *Proposition 11* on this subject. Then, to explain "the theological motivation for the ecclesiastical law on celibacy", he writes: "The will of the Church finds its ultimate motivation in the *link between celibacy and Sacred Ordination*, which configures the priest to Jesus Christ the Head and Spouse of the Church. The Church as the Spouse of Jesus Christ wishes to be loved by the priest in the total and exclusive manner in which Jesus Christ her Head and Spouse loved her."

NOTES

1. Christian Cochini, *Origines apostoliques du célibat sacerdotal* (Le Sycomore), *Culture et vérité*, Lethielleux/Namur, Paris 1981. On the much debated problem of celibacy in the Church today, see a special number of the review *Concilium: Le Célibat du Sacerdoce catholique*, in *Concilium* 78 (1972).
2. A.M. Stickler, in Cochini, (*ut supra*), *Préface*, p. 6.
3. H. Crouzel, *Une nouvelle étude sur les origines du célibat ecclésiastique*, in *Bull. de Litt. eccl.* 83 (1982), 293-297.
4. See also two studies by canonists: P. Pampaloni, *Continenza e celibato del clero. Leggi e motivi delle fonti canoniche dei secoli IV e V*, in *Studia Patavina* 17 (1970), 5-59; J. Coriden, *Célibat, Droit canonique et Synode 1971*, in *Concilium* 78 (1972), 101-114.

5. See our article *Mari d'une seule femme. Le sens théologique d'une formule paulinienne*, in *Paul de Tarse, apôtre de notre temps* (ed. L. De Lorenzi), Rome 1979, 619-638. In the present study we confine ourselves to the Latin tradition; as is well known, a different discipline obtains in the Oriental Churches.

6. A.M. Stickler, *L'évolution de la discipline du célibat dans l'Église en occident de la fin de l'âge patristique au Concile de Trente*, in *Sacerdoce et célibat. Études historiques et théologiques* (ed. J. Coppens), Gembloux-Louvain 1971, pp. 373-442.

7. Cochini, *op. cit.*, pp. 5-6.

8. See our study *Mari d'une seule femme*, (*ut supra*), p. 635, n. 64, where we show that the formula *unius uxoris vir* (1 Tim 3:2) expresses the marriage relationship of the covenant between God and his people, between Christ the bridegroom and his bride the Church. Furthermore, the similarity of the formula in 1 Tim 3:2 with the one nearby in 1 Tim 2:5: *unus Deus, unus... homo Christus Iesus* permits the connection to be made with the prophetic theme of the covenant, and to uncover a link with the Old Testament; cf especially Mal 2:14 (LXX): 'the *wife* of your *covenant*'; 2:10: 'the covenant of our forefathers'.

9. A.M. Stickler, in Cochini, (*ut supra*), *Préface*, pp. 5-6 (our italics).

10. Cf our article *La struttura di alleanza del sacerdozio ministeriale*, in *Communio* 112 (July-August 1990), 102-114, where we summarise the results of the previous study: *Mari d'une seule femme*, (*vide supra*), in order to apply them specifically both to the case of priestly celibacy and to that of the priesthood of men (not of women).

11. For this historical part, see the texts in Cochini, *op. cit.*, pp. 19-26.

12. The text (taken from CCL 149, 13) is given in the original Latin with a French translation in Cochini, *op. cit.*, pp. 25-26.

13. For the decretal *Cum in unum* of Pope Siricius, cf *Ep.* V, c. 9 (PL 13, 1161 A); it is also found in the African Council of Theleptis (AD 418): *Conc. Thelense* (CCL 149, 62): French trans.: Cochini, *op. cit.*, p. 32; see also the two letters of Pope Innocent I (AD 404-405) to the bishops Victricius of Rouen and Exuperius of Toulouse: *Ep.* II, (PL 20, 476 A. 497 B; Cochini, *op. cit.*, pp. 284-286). Africa, Spain and the Gauls thus take direction as indicated by the Popes.

14. Cochini, *op. cit.*, p. 33 (our italics).

15. For P. Pampaloni for instance (*art. cit.*, 41-42), this would involve "a forced interpretation of the Apostle"; he does however concede that, according to the sources of the period, that interpretation was probably regarded as the correct one. H. Crouzel (*art. cit.*, 294) also rightly observes: if it were true, as these Fathers thought, that the Apostle regarded 'monogamy' as guaranteeing suitability for continence, we should then have to suppose that, for Paul, it was a known fact "either that the wife was dead or that the candidate was to live with her as with a sister: which unfortunately the Pauline text does not make clear." This

is true. But the Pauline text does contain a literary contact with 2 Cor 11:2 (*vide infra*), which allows the indirect recovery of the theme of continence as a covenantal theme.

16. Cf our article *Mari d'une seule femme*, *(art. cit)*: 'I. Histoire de d'exégèse' (pp. 620-623); 'II. Insuffisance des deux interprétations en présence' (pp. 624-628).

17. Stickler, *L'évolution de la discipline du célibat, (ut supra)*, pp. 441-442.

18. Cf *Ad uxorem*, I, 7, 4 (CCL 1, 381); the reference here is to 1 Tim 3:2, 12; Tit 1:6; see too *De exhort. cast.*, 7, 2 (CCL 2, 1024).

19. *De exhort. cast.*, 13, 4 (CCL 2, 1035): on this passage, see Cochini's comment, *op. cit.*, pp. 168-171.

20. *Ibid.*, cf *Ad uxorem*, 1, 4, 4, speaking of women who, instead of choosing a husband, have preferred a virginal life: *"Malunt enim Deo nubere. Deo speciosae, Deo sunt puellae"* (CCL 1, 377).

21. *De virg. vel.*, 16, 4: *"Nupsisti enim Christo, illi tradidisti carnem tuam, illi sponsasti maturitatem tuam"* (CCL 2, 1225); *De res.*, 61, 6: *"virgines Christi maritae"* (CCL 2, 1010).

22. *De monog.*, 5, 7 (CCL 2, 1235)

23. *De exhort. cast.*, 5, 3 (CCL 2, 1023); hence, Tertullian goes on, the law of single marriage is also founded on *'Christi sacramentum'*.

24. The Apostle thus in no way excludes the 'carnal' use of marriage between Christian husbands and wives, despite what Tertullian the Montanist was to pretend to the contrary, cf *De exhort. cast.*, 9, 3 (CCL 2, 1028): for the latter, marriage as such (not a second marriage) was to be regarded as a sort of *stuprum*. As can be seen from this brief analysis, *'una caro'* (Eph 5:31) and *'una uxor'* (1 Tim 3:2) have very different functions, although the same adjective *una* occurs in both texts: Tertullian's mistake was to have virtually identified them: 'una *caro*' undoubtedly legitimizes *conjugal relations*; whereas 'una *uxor*', as we shall see, excludes them, and instead becomes the theological basis for *continence*.

25. St Augustine speaks of this in the *De coniugiis adulterinis*, II, 20, 22: *"solemus eis proponere continentiam clericorum"* (PL 40, 486).

26. *De bono coniugali*, 18, 21 (PL 40, 387-388).

27. *De continentia*, 9, 23 (PL 40, 364).

28. Stickler, *L'évolution... (ut supra)*, p. 381; sundry texts from penitential books are quoted in the notes.

29. St Leo the Great, *Ep. ad Rusticum Narbonensem episc. Inquis. III: Resp.* (PL 54, 1204 A): *"ut de carnali fiat spirituale coniugium"*.

30. Cf J. Daniélou, *La jalousie de Dieu*, in *Dieu vivant*, n. 4, 16 (1950), 61-73.

31. Cf our work *Mary in the Mystery of the Covenant*, New York 1992, pp. xxiii-xxv, xxxv-xxxvii.

32. Cf R. Hesbert, *Saint Augustin et la virginité de la foi*, in *Augustinus*

29

Magister. Congrès international augustinien (Paris, Sept. 1954), II, Paris 1954, pp. 645-655.

33. St Leo the Great, *Epistolae*, 12, 3 (PL 54, 648 B).
34. E. Tauzin, *Note sur un texte de Saint Paul (Essai d'exégèse synthétique)* in *Revue apologétique* 36 (1924-1925), 274-289 (see p. 289, in the note). It should be noted that this author too has spontaneously made the connection between the formular *unius uxoris vir* of the Pastoral Letters and the *virgo casta* of 2 Cor 11:2.
35. *In 1 ad Tim.*, c. III, lect. 1 (ed. Marietti 1953, n. 96); see too Denis the Carthusian, on 1 Tim 3:12 (*Opera omnia*, 13, 420).

Priestly celibacy in patristics and in the history of the Church

Roman Cholij

Secretary of the Apostolic Exarch for Ukrainian Catholics in
Great Britain

It is clear from the New Testament (Mk 1:29-31; Mt 8:14-15; Lk 4:38-39; 1 Tim 3:2, 12; Tit 1:6) that at least the Apostle Peter had been married, and that bishops, presbyters and deacons of the Primitive Church were often family men. It is also clear from epigraphy, the testimony of the Fathers, synodal legislation, papal decretals and other sources that in the following centuries, a married clergy, in greater or lesser numbers was a normal feature of the life of the Church. Even married popes are known to us.[1] And yet, paradoxically, one has to desist, when faced with this incontrovertible fact, from assuming that this necessarily excluded the co-existence of an obligatory celibacy discipline.

In the patristic era, clerical celibacy, strictly speaking meant the inability to enter marriage once a higher Order had been received. The first legislative expression of this is found in the eastern councils of Ancyra (314), c. 10, and Neocaesarea (ca. 314-325), c. 1, for deacons and priests respectively. An Armenian collection of canons, probably from 365, includes this prohibition of marriage[2] and it is clearly expressed in the Apostolic Constitutions and Apostolic Canons of the late fourth century.[3] Canon 14 of the Ecumenical Council of Chalcedon (451) likewise endorses this discipline (albeit indirectly), and it is found in other documents of the fifth and subsequent centuries which consider the practice to be an ancient and timeless tradition.[4]

At first sight this insistence, with its serious canonical penalties, on the law of what would eventually be called the "impediment of orders to contracting marriage" is curious for its apparent lack of scriptural foundation. At best there is the injunction from the Pastoral epistles, "man of one wife" (1 Tim 3:2, 12; Tit 1:6), which would prohibit only a widower cleric from remarrying, but in actual fact this was generally interpreted by patristic authorities as being a prohibition of ordaining remarried laymen.[5] Theodore of Mopsuestia and Theodoret of Cyrrhus stand apart, however, in that they do attest to a different tradition of interpretation. St Paul, according to them, was concerned only with marital fidelity and not with a prohibition of ordaining the remarried.[6] Nonetheless, the tendency was to understand strict monogamy as being, together with other qualities required of the wife, a guarantee that the future deacon or priest would be able to live chastely.[7]

Among the legislators of the West, there seems to be a curious lack of interest, given the legislative activity of the East, in the matter of contracting marriage after ordination. Among individual authors the first hint of this rule is in the *Philosophoumena* of Hippolytus of Rome (d. 235) where Pope Callistus is accused of unforgivable innovations in ecclesiastical discipline, including the ordination of the remarried. Hippolytus then adds: "And even if a member of the clergy did marry, he could, as far as Callistus was concerned, remain a cleric, as if he had not sinned".[8] Indirectly, and independently of the truth of these accusations, we learn of what, in the author's mind, was the traditional discipline. A further reference is found in the *Quaestiones Veteris et Novi Testamenti* of Ambrosiaster who lived under the pontificate of Pope Damasus (366-84). He writes, a propos of objections to priestly continence, "But people might say: if it is permitted and good to marry, why should priests not be authorized to take wives? In other words, why should ordained men not be permitted to be united (to wives)?"[9] The significance of the second sentence of this quotation, in relation to the first, can be better appreciated if read in the light of a Roman document of the following century. Pope Leo the Great writes to Bishop Rusticus of Narbonne (458/9):

> The law of continence is the same for the ministers of the altar, for the bishops and for the priests; when they were (still) lay people or lectors, they could freely take a wife and beget children. But once they have reached the ranks mentioned above, what had been permitted is no longer so.[10]

Introduced here is the technical expression 'law of continence' (*lex continentiae*). It can also be called the law of celibacy in a 'wide' sense. Early Western legislation tends to focus on clerical continence as specifically applied to married clergy: the discipline of abstinence from marital relations. If a bishop, priest or deacon (and subdeacon from the fifth century onwards) was prohibited from having sexual relations once in orders, then it is obvious that his commitment to continence would be the major impediment to subsequent marriage (quite apart from the general disfavour shown towards second marriage). For there could be no real marriage unless it was potentially open to sexual consummation. The same law of continence would also impede the unmarried deacon or priest from marrying. The laws, so clearly expressed in the East, prohibiting marriage to the already ordained may thus be reasonably understood to be but the reverse expression of this more basic discipline of continence. This possibility needs to be taken into account when reconstructing the history of clerical celibacy.

Although perhaps strange to our own modern ways of thinking, absolute marital continence was far from unknown or unesteemed in patristic times. Tertullian, himself a married man, informs us in his Catholic period, of lay people who practise continence within marriage *"pro cupiditate regni coelestis"*.[11] So do Jerome and Augustine in the following century.[12] The rapid growth of monasticism and an attraction to the ascetic life led many couples to

33

renounce their intimacy and to enter a monastery[13] or to live in continence within more domestic settings. Church authorities had to intervene decisively when the enthusiasm for continence was deemed excessive and tainted with heretical motives, but at the same time praising those who lived the life of continence for the right motives.[14] Four centuries later the Second Nicene Council (787) would still endorse the possibility of monastic vocations for the married.[15] Neither should one forget the continence that the separated and divorced were required to live. Augustine did not hesitate to invoke the example of some of the married clergy, who had had their difficulties in adjusting to a life of continence, in order to encourage men separated from their wives to live continently. He also applies the celibacy *logion* "eunuchs for the sake of the kingdom of heaven" (Mt 19:12) to divorcees.[16]

Clerical continence in the West

a. Fourth century legislation

Convincing testimonies to the normative nature of clerical continence in the fourth century can be found in individual Western patristic authors (such as Ambrose, Augustine, Jerome). The first known example of actual legislation is c. 33 of the Spanish Council of Elvira, the usual date of which is given as ca. 305. It reads:

We decree that all bishops, priests and deacons in the service of the ministry are entirely forbidden to have conjugal relations with their wives and to beget children; should anyone do so, let him be excluded from the honour of the clergy.[17]

There is a similar canon which certain manuscripts ascribe to the First Council of Arles (314), considered to be a sort of General Council of the West. Canon 29 reads:

Moreover, (concerned with) what is worthy, pure, and honest, we exhort our brothers (in the episcopate) to make sure that priests and deacons have no (sexual) relations with their wives, since they are serving the ministry every day. Whoever will act against this decision, will be deposed from the honour of the clergy.[18]

The wording of these canons does not immediately suggest that an innovation is being introduced, and it would be an error in historical procedure to maintain *a priori* that such was the case. The seriousness of the implications for the life of the clergy, the absence of justification for the strictness of the discipline and the canonical penalty attached, would suggest, on the contrary, that the Church authorities were concerned with the *maintenance* and not the introduction of this rule. The important papal decretals of the fourth century, which indicate the rule for all the West – *Directa* (385) and *Cum in unum* (386) of Pope Siricius; *Dominus inter* of Innocent I (or Damasus?), and the Synod of Carthage (390) – were in fact emphatic that clerical continence belonged to immemorial, even apostolic, tradition.[19] Patristic writings are often explicit in considering the apostles as models of the priesthood. Yet those who might have been married were thought not to have lived other than in continence.[20]

b. The fifth to the seventh centuries

As with other juridical institutions of the Church, with time clerical continence developed sharper and more defined outlines. From the fifth to the seventh centuries much provincial conciliar activity is seen in the West where both the obligation to continence is reaffirmed (indicating infringement), and greater precision, taking into account changed circumstances, is given to the law. Canonical collections would circulate and consciousness of legislating in conformity with a wider legal patrimony and with ancient tradition is sometimes made explicit.[21]

One of the interesting features of legislation that appears throughout this period is the implicit or even explicit inclusion of a continent wife among that class of women that c. 3 of the First Ecumenical Council of Nicaea (325) had characterized as beyond suspicion: "The great Council has absolutely forbidden bishops, priests and deacons – in other words, all the members of the clergy – to have with them a sister-companion (*syneisaktos*) with the exception of a mother, a sister, an aunt, or, lastly, only those persons who are beyond any suspicion." The wife, like the husband, was technically 'converted', *conversio* being the change of life that follows on the profession or public promise of continence.[22] It is in mid-fifth century Gaul that an explicit public declaration of the commitment to continence first appears.[23] This was to prevent excuses of ignorance of the obligation which previously had been implicit in the reception of orders. The wife (who in the Gallic Church was termed a *presbytera, diaconissa, subdiaconissa* or even *episcopia* according to the status of her husband)[24] was to live as a 'sister' in a brother-sister relationship.[25] Her rights were protected as ordination could not go ahead without her agreement.[26] Her promise to live in continence was also an impediment to future marriage.[27]

Cohabitation of husband and wife had been given the explicit backing of papal authority. Leo the Great wrote in 458-9: "...in order for the union (of bishops, priests, deacons) to change from carnal to spiritual, they must, without sending away their wives, live with them as if they did not have them, so that conjugal love be safeguarded and nuptial activity cease."[28] Fifth and sixth century imperial legislation also endorses cohabitation, although without specifying its nature,[29] as does the Eastern Apostolic Canon 6(5): "Let no bishop, priest or deacon send his spouse away under the pretext of piety...", part of a collection of canons, of Syrian or Palestinian origin, which had considerable influence on the Churches of the fifth and sixth centuries. The Byzantine Church, at the end of the seventh century, would interpret this canon as authorizing marital relations.

Continent cohabitation expressed trust in the nobility of human love to combine marital affection with the values of the consecrated clerical state. Paulinus of Nola (d. 431) and Pseudo-Jerome (ca. 417?) indicate a warm spirituality for those embracing this new life.[30] Yet the difficulties of the discipline were not unappreciated by the Church authorities. The necessary conditions for this life was a constant concern, Pope Gregory the Great deeming it "harsh and inopportune" (*durum atque incompetens*) to expect its observance from the unprepared.[31] A return to conjugal relations, after all, was often considered to be as serious a sin as adultery,[32] the cleric being punished by reduction to the lay state. Councils also occupied themselves with the details of sleeping arrangements to avoid possible scandal to the faithful.[33] A shortage of vocations due to the rapid growth of the Church was not to be taken as an excuse for mitigating traditional rules.[34] Finally, because of the real possibilities of incontinence, and departing from earlier practice, total physical separation would be recommended[35] or even sometimes required.[36]

Clerical continence in the East

1. Patristic testimonies

Any direct evidence for rules or customs of marital continence in the East comes from patristic writers rather than from Councils. However, one must bear in mind the possible implicit presence of the rule in the tradition of the impediment of orders to contracting marriage. The Persian Church (which was outside the Byzantine Empire and became Nestorian) did, however, legislate, in the late fifth century, explicitly *against* the practice of clerical marital continence, at the same time authorizing those already in

37

orders to contract marriage. The Council of Mar Acacius (486), which ratified a similar decision of the Council of Beth Lafath (484), recognized the *antiquity* of these traditions of celibacy, but abrogated them, rather than as in the West, try to reinforce them. The Council did this in an effort to eradicate or regularize clerical incontinence.[37] The previous obligatory character of continence is strongly implied, as is the intrinsic relationship between continence and the impediment of orders.

Eusebius of Caesarea, a prominent bishop at the Council of Nicaea, writes in the *Demonstratio Evangelica*, I, 9 (315-325): "It is fitting, according to Scripture, 'that a bishop be the husband of an only wife'. But this being understood, it behoves consecrated men, and those who are at the service of God's cult, to abstain thereafter from conjugal intercourse with their wives." St Jerome, who had a good knowledge of the Eastern Churches, writes to the priest Vigilantius (406): "What would the Eastern Churches do? What would (those of) Egypt and the Apostolic See do, they who never accept clerics unless they are virgins or continent men, or if they had had a wife, (accept them only) if they give up matrimonial life..." (*Adversus Vigilantium*, 2).

Epiphanius (315-403), born in Palestine and consecrated bishop of Constantia in Cyprus, condemns all forms of encratism but nonetheless insists that priests themselves are required to live continently, as regulated (he believed) by the apostles. Priestly continence is observed, he maintains, wherever the ecclesiastical canons are adhered to, human weakness and the shortage of vocations being inadequate reasons for clergy to contravene the rule.[38]

Synesius of Ptolemais, of the Libyan Church, knows that he is expected to live in continence with his wife if made bishop,[39] and Palladius the historian reports that a synod presided over by John Chrysostom, Bishop of Constantinople in the year 400, condemned Antoninus, Bishop of Ephesus, for doing what was forbidden by the 'holy laws' including resuming common life with his wife.[40]

Other testimonies to be taken into special account include Origen (d. ca. 253) (*23rd homily on Numbers, 6th homily on Leviticus*), Ephraem Syrus (*Carmina Nisibena*, 18 and 19 [ca. 363]), and the Syriac *Doctrina Addei* (ca. 400).

Caution, of course, has to be exercised in not reading into these texts more than they contain, and one has to recognize that local practices do not necessarily imply a general rule. Furthermore, other tests need to be considered, such as Clement of Alexandria, *Stromata* III, 12; Cyril of Jerusalem, *Catechesis* 12, 25; Athanasius, *Letter to Dracontius* which do not obviously suggest the possibility of a general rule. Indeed, since the end of the nineteenth century such texts have been used to demonstrate the existence of an early general law of continence in the East. Polemical or confessional interests aside, it can be said that modern tools of scholarship, not available in the past, have allowed doubt to be cast on the certainty of these conclusions too.[41]

b. Legislation tothe seventh century

The only law dealing with continence promulgated at the Council of Nicaea was canon 3, dealing with the categories of women a cleric was permitted to live with. The famous story of Bishop Paphnutius of Egypt, first recounted by the Greek historian Socrates in the mid-fifth century, relates how at the Council a proposal to impose obligatory clerical continence on all the Churches was opposed by the bishop and then rejected.[42] But this story has been proved to be a myth, without any historical foundation.[43] Socrates' statement (*HE*, V, 22) that continence was a voluntary matter in the East, and the bishops were held to no law prohibiting them to continue having children, is likewise unreliable.[44]

Canon 10 of Ancyra (314) allows the marriage of a deacon if he makes known his desire at ordination, otherwise it is forbidden. This exception was not accepted by the Chalcedonian Christian Churches (Chalcedon [451], c. 14) and recently doubts have been raised over the authenticity of the canon in its present formulation.[45] Canon 8 of Neocaesarea (314-325) requires the expulsion from the clerical home of an adulterous wife, yet a similar law was found in the West within the setting of clerical continence.[46] Gangra (ca. 340), c. 4, anathematized those who refused to receive communion from a married priest and c. 6 of the Apostolic Canons, from the late fourth century, prohibited sending a wife away under the pretext of piety. Canon 51 (not accepted as authentic in the West) deposed a cleric who kept continence for heretical reasons rather than from 'personal discipline'. The background to these laws was the rejection of heretical encratism, and nothing certain can be said concerning the authorisation (or otherwise) of marital relations in these canons.

Emperor Justinian, on the other hand, considers priestly continence to be the rule, even if it is not always observed. Writing of those clerics who contract marriage after orders, he states: "...some of them (i.e., priests, deacons, subdeacons) despise the holy canons and beget children from the wives with whom, according to the priestly rule, they are not permitted to have relations."[47] Children born after ordination were declared illegitimate. The Emperor also went further than the ecclesiastical canons in requiring bishops to be without progeny, for fear of alienation of Church property.[48] Bishops would thus preferably be chosen from the ranks of unmarried clerics and monks.[49] Childless married bishops were to live away from their wives.[50]

The Quinisext Synod, or Synod 'in Trullo' (691), is of very special significance. It followed Justinian in requiring bishops to be separated from their wives (c. 12). This was to be done by common agreement before their consecration, and the wives would enter a monastery where they could become deaconesses (c. 48). The requirement of childlessness was ignored (this was abrogated by Emperor Leo VI two centuries later). Widespread ignorance among clergy of the laws governing marriage is acknowledged and traditional discipline re-asserted (c. 3). But married priests, deacons and subdeacons are authorized to have marital relations, except during the periods when they serve at the altar (c. 13). Priests in 'barbarian' lands who live in continence are required to separate from their wives (c. 30). With regard to c. 13, which is of special importance to subsequent tradition, two canonical authorities are invoked to authorize marital relations: c. 6 of the Apostolic Canons (with bishops, however, excluded) and the canons of the *Codex Canonum Ecclesiae Africanae*, compiled in 419. The *Codex*, however, is clearly misinterpreted. The canon from the Synod of Carthage (390) which is quoted had declared perpetual continence (...*continentes esse in omnibus*) to be "what the apostles taught and what antiquity itself has observed". Here it is presented as saying the same of 'temporary' continence. The Trullan Synod is regarded in the East as part of the Sixth Ecumenical Council (681-2), thus having supreme legislative authority. It has since remained the definitive statement on clerical marriage. Rome, on the other hand, immediately objected to the canons which were against Western discipline and to this day has not accepted them as belonging to the ecumenical heritage.[51]

Early motives for clerical continence

The Trullan Synod highlights service at the altar as the dominant motive for clerical continence, even if only practised on a temporary basis. Indeed, the patristic theology of the priesthood, stressing its intercessorial and mediatorial function favoured, on scriptural grounds, a connection between dedicated continence and priestly prayer.[52] The abstinence recommended by St Paul in 1 Corinthians 7:5, in order to devote oneself to prayer, was one such scriptural ground. This also figured prominently in the history of married lay spirituality. A further prominent argument, appearing first in the fourth century papal decretals and in St Ambrose, was a counter-argument to the 'judaizing' argument of those priests unwilling to embrace continence. These justified their behaviour by calling upon the exam-

41

ple of the Levites of the Old Testament. The swift response was that the Christian priesthood was more than a continuation of the Levitical priesthood – it was its perfection, being spiritual and non-hereditary. Hence the *a fortiori* case: if the Levites practised temporary continence when in the sanctuary, so much more should Christian priests, always ready to serve, practise continence.[53]

One scriptural quotation notable for its absence in the early texts is the Matthean *logion*: "eunuchs for the sake of the kingdom" (Mt 19:12), which is never directly applied to priests. This omission suggests an attitude that priestly continence was not to be considered a voluntary perfection of the priestly state, but rather to be an intrinsic characteristic. Pope Siricius (385) called its relation to priesthood 'indissoluble'.[54] Subsequent Western canonical tradition, by its refusal to mitigate the law, seems to have displayed a similar conviction.

It is true that, in the patristic age, the marked sense of the transcendence of God led to an anthropology that relativized many of the values of marriage to the things of this world. Relative to the things of God, sexual activity could be described in terms that draw on the vocabulary of Levitical ritualism but which offend the linguistic sensibilities of our own time.[55] And yet it would be wrong to see in this use of language a veiled encratism, and in the discipline of priestly continence an attack on marriage. The fact that married men, with sexual experience, were chosen for the ministry showed the Church's respect towards conjugal values.[56] The new exclusive relationship to the Church inherent in the nature of priestly ordination would mean, however, that thenceforth the type of exclusivity implicit in sexual relations had to be renounced.[57]

The Eastern Churches from the seventh century

The mandatory norms of continence for Byzantine married priests following the Trullan Synod were generally patterned after the norms that then existed for married lay people: one to three days of 'eucharistic' continence as well as continence during the periods of fasting.[58] Reception of communion was not frequent among the faithful during the Middle Ages; the continence rule also discouraged attempts by married priests to celebrate the Eucharist daily. Non-monastic priests were expected to be married. From the eleventh century norms appear which prohibit the ordination to the parochial ministry of an unmarried man. Those celibates who worked closely with the bishop would be unmarried priests who had taken the monastic profession. Thus arose, in later Russia, the distinction between the 'black'-(monastic) clergy and the 'white' (parochial) clergy. Those married clergy who became widowers were compelled to leave their ministry and enter a monastery. The Synod of Moscow (1666-1667) abrogated this requirement, at the same time authorizing remarriage with reduction to the state of a minor cleric. Bishops, in keeping with the spirit, if not the letter, of Trullan legislation, were chosen from amongst monastic candidates, although, exceptionally, a celibate layman would be ordained after making monastic profession.

More research is needed to understand properly the developments in the non-Chalcedonian Churches under Islamic rule. It is reasonable to assume, however, that whilst under Byzantine rule imperial legislation was required to be observed. By the High Middle Ages a tradition had developed in the Coptic Church of ordaining children to the diaconate. They were permitted to marry after reaching puberty. The Nestorians, who were outside the Empire, continued from the fifth century to have a married clergy not bound to strict continence. All Orthodox Churches today have a married clergy.

The Eastern Churches in union with Rome followed the norms of temporary continence appropriate to each respective tradition. The ordination of unmarried men was encouraged by the Eastern hierarchies, bishops also being selected from non-monastic candidates. The discipline of temporary continence has been largely ignored in the twentieth century, presumably because of the assimilation to contemporary Roman Catholic practice of daily Eucharist. Special decrees have been issued by the Holy See in respect to married clergy outside the territory of origin of their Church, and the present law is found in the *Codex Canonum Ecclesiarum Orientalium*.

The Western Church from the seventh century

From the seventh century to the time of the Gregorian Reform and the legislation of the Lateran Councils, Church authorities made constant efforts to reform clerical mores. The whole fabric of clerical life, not just the life of continence, was deeply affected by the new social structures and changed conditions that followed the disintegration of imperial organization. The tone of the disciplinary measures taken by the hierarchy was that of conservation and reformation, not innovation. Canonical collections, such as the *Dionysiana*, were circulated widely, reminding bishops of the discipline of earlier centuries. Some over-zealous reformers skilfully fabricated a number of texts, claiming they had been lost, to add even greater weight to the existing sources. These formed part of the *Pseudo-Isidorian Forgeries* (ca. 850), the decretals of which had particular influence. They were accepted because of the widely-held conviction that they corresponded to the spirit of traditional legislation. Penitential books and the *Capitularies* of the Frankish bishops also expressed the need to conserve established discipline, as did the rulings of many regional councils and diocesan synods as well as the interventions of the popes.[59] Patristic sources are sometimes quoted by councils and some, such as the Council of Metz (888) and the Council of Mainz (888), prohibited cohabitation even with wives living in continence.

The Gregorian Reform, enthusiastically encouraged by the monasteries, was a systematic effort to strike at the

roots of abuses in the Church. It was directed against si-
mony, 'Nicolaitism' (priests living in marriage) and also
lay investiture. The success of the Reform was largely due
to the uninhibited exercise of papal authority, by Gregory
VII and his successors, over the bishops who had allowed
traditional discipline to be ignored or forgotten. This period is also characterized by the appearance of theoretical
attacks on priestly celibacy, with corresponding counter-
arguments: the *libelli de lite*. One argument used by the
opponents to the reform was the story of Paphnutius at the
Council of Nicaea. Gregory VII condemned this at the
Roman Synod of 1077 as a falsification of history.

Of the numerous synods convoked throughout Europe
during the eleventh and twelfth centuries to enforce with
rigour the neglected law, the most notable are the First
Lateran Council (1123) and the Second Lateran Council
(1139), considered as ecumenical in Roman tradition.
Lateran I made into general law the prohibition of cohabit-
ing with wives (c. 7). Lateran II, c. 7, reiterating the declaration of the Council of Pisa (1135), also declared marriages
contracted subsequent to ordination to be not only prohibited, but non-existent (... *matrimonium non esse censemus*).
At times, this Council is wrongly interpreted as having
introduced for the first time the general law of celibacy,
with only unmarried men being admitted to the priesthood.
Yet what the Council was doing, in a more pointed way,
was re-emphasizing the law of *continence* (... *ut autem lex
continentiae et Deo placens munditia in ecclesiasticis
personis et sacris personis dilatetur*...).[60] Subsequent legislation, however, continues to deal with questions relating
to married men ordained *secundum legem*, not *contra legem*.

The principle sources for this legislation are the *Quinque
Compilationes Antiquae* and the decretals of Gregory IX.
These decretals form part of the *Corpus Iuris Canonici*, a
work completed in the fourteenth century and which influ-
enced law-making until the appearance of the 1917 *Code of
Canon Law*. From these sources, we learn that from the
time of Alexander III (1159-1181) married men were not,

as a rule, allowed to have ecclesiastical benefices; a lower cleric who married would have his benefice withdrawn, but not his right to subdiaconate ordination on the condition that he discontinues his marital life. A son of a priest (considered legitimate if born before ordination) was prohibited from succeeding to his father's benefice. Young wives and the wives of bishops were to agree at the time of ordination to enter a convent.[61] The rights of the wife were also protected.

In 1322 Pope John XXII insisted that no one bound in marriage – even if unconsummated – could be ordained unless there was full knowledge of the requirements of Church law. If the free consent of the wife had not been obtained, the husband, even if already ordained, was to be reunited with his wife, exercise of his ministry being barred.[62] One of the factors that must have contributed to the eventual universal practice of ordaining only unmarried men would have been the assumption that a wife would not want to give up her marital rights. Hence the *irregularitas ex defectu libertatis* of a married man, which became a formal impediment (*impedimentum simplex*) only in the twentieth century with the promulgation of the *Codex Iuris Canonici* (1917), was not due to the marriage bond *per se*. It was due to this assumption of unwillingness and inability to separate. From 1917, all cases of dispensation from the impediment were reserved to the Holy See. But those receiving dispensation were not authorized by that fact to continue with marital relations.[63]

The decretals and other parts of the *Corpus Iuris Canonici* provided the guidelines for synodal activity, concubinage being a persistent problem for the authorities. Opposition to the law of the Church was not lacking and occasionally well-respected figures argued for a mitigation of the law to help solve the problems of clerical indiscipline (Panormitanus, at the time of the Council of Basle [1417-1437], for example). The example of the practice of the East was given as a precedent, although it is unlikely that there was a proper understanding of this discipline.[64] Similar calls for mitigation were heard at the time of the Reformation. They included humanists such as Erasmus, theologians such as Cajetan de Vio, and secular authorities with pragmatic and political aims in mind: Charles V, Ferdinand I, Maximilian II. The crisis precipitated by the Reformers was doctrinal as well as disciplinary. Zwingli and Martin Luther made the abolition of clerical celibacy a key element to their reform, but this was also related to the dismantling of the traditional theology of the sacramental priesthood.

In the third and final period of the Council of Trent (1562-3), and despite considerable pressures, all suggestions that the Catholic Church should modify and mitigate its rules of celibacy were rejected. In Session XXIV on 11 November 1563, the Fathers upheld the prohibition of clerical marriage (c. 9), adding (concerning the difficulties): "For God would not deny the gift to those who duly ask for it (the gift of chastity), nor allow us to be tempted beyond our strength." They also rejected the thesis that the marital state should be considered better than that of celibacy (c. 10).[65] The Council, in Session XXIII, also voted in favour of founding seminaries to prepare candidates from their youth for the celibate life. The discipline of continence by this time had meant in practice that only an unmarried man would be ordained. This is also shown in the discussions of the Council, for example when one theologian, Desiderius de S. Martino, concerned by the shortage of priests, suggested the possibility of ordaining married men provided the wives gave consent and that they and their husbands lived in continence. But the measure was not deemed expedient.[66]

The decrees of the Council were not immediately accepted in all nations but with time they did bring about a general observance of the law of celibacy, thanks in no small measure to their provisions for the better training of the clergy. The Enlightenment brought fresh assaults against clerical celibacy and after the First Vatican Council, the Old Catholics, separating themselves from Rome, abolished the rule. Despite the pressures on the Catholic Church

47

to relax the law of celibacy, it has always resisted. Pope Benedict XV declared, in his Consistorial Allocution of 16 December 1920, that the Church considered celibacy to be of such importance that it could never abolish it.[67] Following Vatican II, the Church has made an exception for married deacons of mature age and for individual former non-Catholic clergymen, following a precedent set by Pope Pius XII.[68]

NOTES

1. For example Pope Hormisdas (514-23), father to Pope Silverius, his successor.
2. *Canons of Gregory the Illuminator*, c. 2. A. Mai, *Scriptorum veterum nova collectio*, X, 2 (Rome 1838), p. 269.
3. *Apostolic Constitutions*, VI, 17; *Apostolic Canons*, c. 26 (27).
4. Socrates, *Historia Ecclesiastica*, I, 2 (ca. 440); Council of Mar Acacius (486), c. 3; Emperor Justinian, *Novella* 6 (535), chap. 5; Council in Trullo (691), c. 6.
5. Origen, *Homilia in Lucam,* 17; *Contra Celsum* III, 48; Tertullian, *Ad Uxorem*, I, 7; Clement of Alexandria, *Stromata*, III, 12; Ambrose, *Ep.* 63, 62-63; Jerome, *Adversus Jovinianum*, I, 34; John Chrysostom, *In Epist. ad Timotheum I*, III, X, 1-2; Augustine, *De Bono Coniug.*, 18; Epiphanius, *Adv. Haer.*, 59, 4; *Apostolic Canons*, c. 17.
6. Theordoret of Cyrrhus, *Ep.* 110 to Domnus of Antioch. Theodore of Mopsuestia, *In Epist. ad Timotheum I*, III, 2.
7. Second marriage was always thought of in the early Church as being a concession to incontinence. Some Fathers also interpreted "man of one wife" as being *propter continentiam futuram*; Siricius, *Cum in unum* decretal (*Ad episcopos Africae*); Ambrose, *Ep.* 63, 63; Ambrosiaster, *In Epist. ad Timotheum I*, III, 12-13; Epiphanius, *Adv. Haer.*, 59, 4.
8. *Refutatio omnium haeresium*, IX, 12, 22: GCS 26, 249-50.
9. CSEL 50, 414.
10. *Epist. ad Rusticum Narbonensem episcopum, Inquis, III., Resp.* PL 54, 1204a.
11. *Ad uxorem*, I, 6.
12. Jerome, *Ep.* 49, 2; 49, 5; Augustine, *De Coniug. Adult.*, II, 18 (19), 19 (20).
13. Cf Athanasius, *Letter to Dracontius*, PG 25, 532d-33b.
14. Irenaeus, *Adv. haer.*, 28, 1; Clement of Alexandria, *Stromata*, III; Council of Gangra (ca. 340), cc. 1, 4, 9; Epiphanius, *Adv. Haer.*, 48; 59; Augustine, *De Bono Coniug.*, etc. Useful introductions to this theme

include AA. VV., *Etica sessuale e matrimonio nel cristianesimo delle origini*, Studia part. Mediol. 5, Milan 1976, and P. Brown, *The body and society: men, women and sexual renunciation in early Christianity*, New York – Columbia 1988.

15. Canon 20 reads in part: "If there are persons who wish to renounce the world and follow the monastic life along with their relatives, the men should go off to a male monastery and their wives enter a female monastery, for God is surely pleased with this." N. Tanner SJ (ed), *Decrees of the Ecumenical Councils*, vol. I Sheed & Ward – Georgetown U.P. 1990, pp. 153-4.

16. *De Coniug. Adult.*, II, 20 (21); 18 (19).

17. "*Placuit in totum prohibere episcopis presbyteris et diaconibus positis in ministerio abstinere se a coniugibus suis et non generare filios; quicumque vero fecerit, ab honore clericatus exterminetur*", G. Martinez Díez & F. Rodríguez, *La colección canónica hispana*, Madrid 1984), IV, p. 253.

18. *Corpus Christianorum . Series Latina*, (from now on CC) 148, 25.

19. "The question is not one of ordering new precepts, but we wish through this letter to have people observe those that either through apathy   or laziness on the part of some have been neglected. They are,   however, matters that have been established by apostolic constitution, and , by a constitution of the Fathers." *Cum in unum (Ad episcopos Africae)*: PL 13, 1156a. P. Coustant, *Epistolae Romanorum Pontificum* Paris 1721, p. 562. The African Church declared obligatory continence to be "...what the apostles taught and what antiquity itself observed...", CC 149, p. 13. The important study by Christian Cochini SJ should be noted: *The Apostolic origins of priestly celibacy* (trans. Nelly Marans), Ignatius Press/San Francisco 1990 (original French version: *Origines apostoliques du célibat sacerdotale*, Lethielleux/Paris 1981).

20. Clement of Alexandria, *Stromata*, III, 6; Tertullian, *De Monogamia*, 8, 4; Jerome, *Apologeticum ad Pammachium*, *Ep.* 49 (48), 2, 21; Eusebius of Caesarea, *Demonstratio evangelica*, III, 4, 37; Isidore of Pelusium, *Ep.* III, 176.

21. E.g. Tours I (46): CC 148, 143; Agde (506): CC 148, 196; Orléans (549): CC 148 A, 149; Lyons (538): CC 148 A, 232.

22. Arles II (442-506), cc. 2, 3, 43, 44. CC 148, 114, 122-3.

23. Cf Orange (441), c. 21. CC 148, 84.

24. Tours (567), cc. 13 (12), 20 (19). CC 148 A, 180-1, 183-4. Auxerre (561-605), c. 21. *Ibid.*, 268.

25. Girona (517), c. 6. H.T. Bruns, *Canones Apostolorum et Conciliorum saeculorum IV-VII*, Berlin, 1839, II, 19. Clermont (535), c. 13. CC 148 A, 108. Tours (567), c. 13. *Ibid.*, 180-1.

26. Agde (506), c. 16 "...*etiam uxorum voluntas ita requirenda est...*". CC 148, 201. Toledo II (531), c. 1. Bruns, I, 207-8.

27. Toledo I (400), c. 18; Epaon (517), c. 32; Autun (589), c. 22; Bruns, I,

206; II 171 (= CC 148 A, 32-3), 239. Cf the same law in the Armenian Council of Chahabivan (444), c. 2. Mai, X, 2, 292.

28. *Epist. ad Rusticum Narbonensem episcopum, Inquis., III Resp.* PL 54, 1204a.

29. *Codex Theodosianus*, I, 2; *Codex Justinianus*, I, 3, 19.

30. *Ep.* 44. CSEL 29, 372-7. *De Septem Ordinibus Ecclesiae.* PL 30, 159c-d.

31. *Ep.* I, 42 (a. 591). *Monumenta Germaniae Historica* (MGH), *Gregorii I Papae registrum epistolarum*, I, Berlin 1891), p. 67.

32. Cf Jerome, *Adversus Jovinianum*, I, 34. Penitential books of the eighth century would regularly use the language of adultery. Thus, the *Parisiense*, c. 113: *Si quis clericus vel superioris gradus uxorem habuerit et post clericatum eum agnoverit, sciat se adulterium commisisse.* H.J. Schmitz, *Die Bußbücher und die Bußdisziplin der Kirche*, Mainz, 1883, I, 693.

33. E.g., Orléans (541), c. 17. CC 148 A, 136; Tours (567), c. 20 (19). *Ibid.*, 183-4.

34. Arles IV (524). CC 148 A, 43-4.

35. Toledo III (589), c. 5. Bruns, I, 214.

36. Lyons (583), c. 1. CC 148 A, 232.

37. J.B. Chabot, *Synodicon orientale*, Paris 1902, pp. 303-6.

38. *Adv. Haer.*, 48, 9; 59, 4; *Expositio Fidei*, 21.

39. *Ep.* 105 (ca. 410).

40. *Dialogue on the life of Saint John Chrysostom* (408). PG 47, 48a-9a.

41. The very balanced work of Cochini, *op. cit.*, which challenges the conclusions of scholars such as Funk, Leclercq, Vacandard and Gryson, shows the care with which interpretation has to proceed.

42. *Historia Ecclesiastica*, I, 11. PG 67, 101b-4b.

43. F. Winklemann, "Paphnutios, der Bekenner und Bishof". *Probleme der koptischen Literatur* = Wissenschaftliche Beiträge de Martin-Luther-Universität Halle-Wittenberg 1968, 1 (K2), pp. 145-53. Cf H.G. Beck, in *Byzantinische Zeitschrift* 62 (1969), p. 159; W. Gessel in *Annuarium Historiae Conciliorum* 2 (1970), pp. 422-23. G. Denzler, *Das Papsttum und der Amtszölibat*, I, Stuttgart 1973), pp. 9-10. R. Gryson, "Dix ans de recherches sur les origines du célibat ecclésiastique", *Revue Théologique de Louvain* 11 (1980), pp. 164-5.

44. Cochini, *Apostolic origins*, pp. 320-2.

45. *Ibid.*, pp. 169-177.

46. E.g., Elvira (ca. 305), c. 65; Braga II (572), c. 28.

47. To the prefect Julian, 18 October 530: *Codex Justinianus* I, 3, 44. Cf *Novella* 6 (535), chap. 5.

48. To the prefect Atarbius, 1 March 528: CJ I, 3, 41.

49. *Novella* 6, chap. 1.

50. *Novella* 123 (546), chap. 29.

51. On the canons of the Trullan Synod and subsequent Eastern legislation, cf R. Cholij, *Clerical celibacy in East and West*, Leominster, Fowler Wright/Gracewing 1989 (reprint of "Married clergy and ecclesiastical

continence in light of the Council in Trullo (691)", *Annuarium Historiae Conciliorum* 19 (1987), 71-230; 241-299).

52. Cf Origen, *Homily on Numbers*, XXIII, 3; Siricius, 'Directa' decretal: *Ad Himerium Tarraconensem*; Ambrosiaster, *In Epist. ad Timotheum I*; Synod of Carthage (390); St Ephraem, *Carmina Nisibena*, XVIII; Pope Innocent I, *Epist., ad Victricium episcopum Rothomagensem*, IX.

53. Siricius, *Directa* decretal, PL 13, 1138a-39a, P. Coustant, *Epistolae*, pp. 629-31, Ambrose, *De officiis ministrorum*, PL 16, 104b-5a.

54. *Ibid* 1139a.

55. In the *Ad Gallos episcopos* or *Dominus Inter* decretal, the Roman Pontiff (Innocent or Damasus?) states: "...if intercourse is defiling (*pollutio*), it is obvious that the priest must be ready to carry out his celestial functions... so that he himself not be found impure", PL 13, 1186a; P. Coustant, *Epistolae*, pp. 691.

56. Cf Ambrosiaster, *Quaestiones Veteris et Novi Testamenti*, 127. CSEL 50, 414-5. The author explains the relative nature of the concept of 'impurity'.

57. The Church becomes a spiritual wife. Pseudo-Jerome, *De septem ordinibus Ecclesiae*; cf Ephraem, *Carmina Nisibena*, XIX; Chalcedon (451), c. 14 (sixth century rubric): N. Tanner, *Decrees of the Ecumenical Councils*, I, p. 98.

58. For a fuller discussion on the matters raised in this section, cf R. Cholij, *Clerical celibacy in East and West*, pp. 106-179.

59. A.M. (Card.) Stickler, *The evolution of the discipline of celibacy in the Western Church from the end of the patristic era to the Council of Trent*, J. Coppens (ed.), *Priesthood and celibacy*, Milan/Rome 1971, pp. 503-597 (transl. from *Sacerdoce et célibat: Etudes historiques et théologiques (Bibl. Eph. Theol. Lov.)*, Louvain 1971).

60. N. Tanner, *Decrees of the Ecumenical Councils*, I, p. 198. For a more detailed treatment of the significance of the Lateran canons, cf R. Cholij, "De lege coelibatus sacerdotalis: nova investigationis elementa", *Periodica de re morali canonica liturgica*, 78 (1989), pp. 157-185.

61. X, III, 32, c. 6. The main sections of the decretals to be consulted are: Liber III, tit. 1 (*De vita et honestate clericorum*), tit. 2 (*De cohabitatione clericorum et mulierum*), tit. 3 (*De clericis coniugatis*), tit. 32 (*De conversione coniugatorum*), Liber IV, tit. 6 (*Qui clerici vel voventes matrimonium contrahere possunt*).

62. *Extravagantes Joannis XXII, VI, de voto et voti redemptione, cap. un.*

63. B. Ojetti, *Commentarium in Codicem Iuris Canonici*, Rome/P.U.G., 1930), II, pp. 103-109; M.C. a Coronata, *Compendium Iuris Canonici* (Turin/Rome, Marietti, 1949 III, pp. 327-8; F. Capello, *Summa Iuris Canonici* Rome/P.U.G. 1951,), II, pp. 277-8.

64. The *Decretum Gratiani*, part of the *Corpus Iuris Canonici*, gave inaccurate information on the background to Eastern discipline. Cholij, *Clerical celibacy*, pp. 63-4.

65. N. Tanner, *Decrees of the Ecumenical Councils*, II, p. 755.
66. *Concilium Tridentinum Diariorum*, Friburgi Brisgoviae 1924), IX, vi, p. 441.
67. *Acta Apostolicae Sedis* 12 (1920), p. 585.
68. For the implications in present law, cf R. Cholij, "Observaciones criticas acerca de los cánones que tratan sobre el celibato en el Código de Derecho Canónico de 1983", *Ius Canonicum* 31 (1991), pp. 291-305.

The theological basis for priestly celibacy

Max Thurian

Theologian

Christ never married. His life is valid justification for the vocation to celibacy. Jesus Christ calls the laws of creation and of nature into question; he calls into question the law of the Old Covenant which sought to re-establish order in creation and in nature which had been disturbed by sin.

He does not, of course, abolish the order of creation, the laws of nature and the law of Moses but completes them all, conferring on these laws their deep, original meaning, a demanding, absolute sign, i.e., the ethics of the Sermon on the Mount. That description of life in the kingdom, unrealizable on earth, is, you might say, a summons to perfection. We must stretch out to what we can only realize at the end, in life eternal. From time to time we hear ourselves called and condemned by Christ's absolute proposition, and this inspires us with real humility, with a sense of our own deep wretchedness and an ardent yearning for Jesus Christ's return. This absolute leads to a morality of rupture and sacrifice. It is not possible to order life by means of the law and to canalize the passions by moral precept. As followers of Christ, we must aim for that pure love which renounces life. "You have heard that it was said: 'You shall not commit adultery'. But I say to you that everyone who looks at a woman lustfully has already committed adultery with her in his heart" (Mt 5:27-28). Who can escape adultery down in the depths of his heart? The law has become an absolute, at the same time attracting us and judging us. No one who wants to obey Christ can go on wanting this world and the order of creation and the natural order to last for ever; we look forward to the end: "Come, Lord Jesus". In waiting for this return, we must not lapse into discouragement and despair. With the help of the Holy Spirit and in vigilant perseverance sustained by prayer and self-discipline, we can indeed win victories. We shall seek our strength in Christ and accept that we have to make breaks with the world. Immediately after extending adultery to the most secret desires of the heart, Jesus goes on as follows: "If your eye causes you to sin, pluck it out and throw it away; it is better that you lose one of your members than that your whole body be thrown into hell..." (Mt 5:29-30). Waiting for Christ to return and make us holy, we have to live in the world and, to give significance to this waiting and make it something real, we ought to accept sacrifice in our lives.

The offering of priestly celibacy

Celibacy is one of those signs that reminds us of Christ's absolute demands, of his liberating return, of the economy of the kingdom of heaven, of the need to be vigilant, to break with the world, with the flesh, with lust, and, with joy in our hearts, to accept renunciation of the passions for pure love of Jesus. Celibacy reminds us that marriage in Christ also entails sacrificial demands: complete and life-long faithfulness (monogamy and indissolubility), and purity of heart (adultery is not merely physical). Celibacy is one way of obeying Christ's invitation: "If any man would come after me, let him deny himself and take up his cross and follow me. For whoever would save his life will lose it, and whoever loses his life for my sake will find it" (Mt 16:24-25).

Observing celibacy for the sake of the kingdom of heaven does not mean being any the less a man; by renouncing a natural form of existence, the priest discovers life in all its fullness. Christ was certainly no less of a man because he did not have affections other than those for his brethren, and a bride other than the Church.

In talking about the vocation to voluntary celibacy, Jesus must have been thinking initially about himself, possibly too about John the Baptist who had preceded him along that road, with his own life thus inaugurating the new order preached by the Messiah. This new order expressed by the celibate lives of John the Baptist and Jesus tells us we need to be in the world without being of the world, "for time is short... let those who deal with the world live as though they had no dealings with it... For the form of this world is passing away" (1 Cor 7:29-31). In what Jesus says about celibacy (cf Mt 19:12), he points out that, in the Christian community, besides the use of natural good things, there is renunciation of them. The order of creation is affirmed by the gospel, but can even so be negated for the sake of the kingdom of God, the new order which is superimposed on the old order of creation. [1]

Hence the use of celibacy, the renunciation of the old order of creation for the new order of the kingdom of heaven, stands in the perspective of the deep demands made by the gospel, "for in the resurrection they neither marry nor are given in marriage, but are like angels in heaven" (Mt 22:30). By celibacy, Jesus – and John the Baptist before him – manifested the ushering in of this new order. "Should we be surprised", Karl Barth writes, "that among the followers of Jesus, then later in the primitive Church, and later still, there were, as it seems, certain men who thought fit to practise this other possibility (this second vocation known as celibacy), men for whom entering to form a part of the Church and living therein, definitely took the place of conjugal union and married life: not out of hostility to marriage understood in the sense of the Letter to the Ephesians 5:31 – marriage restored to all its dignity – but rather because of that reassessment of marriage, and directly inspired by Jesus's own example?"[2]

So, "directly inspired by Jesus's own example", certain

Christians, men and women, in obedience to a divine vocation and also to take advantage of a promise, renounce marriage despite the order of creation faithfully observed by Israel. In the new order of the Last Days, in which we live, God sets certain signs of the kingdom of heaven in his Church, of which celibacy is one. At the beginning of the first Christian century, St Ignatius of Antioch bears witness to the existence of men and women who choose this path "for the honour of God". He writes to Polycarp: "Tell my sisters to love the Lord and to be content with their husbands in the flesh and the spirit. And recommend my brothers to love their wives as the Lord loved the Church (cf Eph 5:25-29). If any of them can persevere in chastity in honour of the Lord's flesh, let them do so without boasting about it."[3]

So St Ignatius relates the celibate state to Christ's human nature, in the perspective of the incarnation which was to usher in a new era. It is consecrated "in honour of the Lord's flesh", in the spirit of imitation and glorification of the life led by Jesus while among us.

When Christ promises a hundredfold to those who have forsaken everything, and especially the possibility of conjugal or family life (... either wives... or children... (Lk 18:29-30)), he is speaking of a renunciation for his sake (or "for the sake of his name" or for the gospel (or "for the sake of the kingdom of God"). And thus he expresses the two main meanings of celibacy, giving it its peculiar character and value. Renunciation of marriage and family, if we are talking of a truly divine gift, has for basic motives love for (for my sake) and the service of God and the Church (for the gospel).

To these first two points we may add a third significance which may be described as 'eschatological'. For it consists in proclaiming the new age of the coming kingdom. When Christ speaks of total renunciation "for the sake of the kingdom of God" (Lk 18:29) or "for the gospel" (Mk 10:29: "for the sake of the good news"), he is not alluding merely to the ministry, to serving the kingdom of

God and the gospel, but also to the new order which he is instituting.

It is impossible to tell what the main meaning of the expression 'for the gospel or the kingdom of God' may be. We have to take the two meanings together, accepting them as complementary to each other. As a result of the good news which gives rise to the new order of the kingdom, some people can no longer live according to the habitual laws of nature and instead devote themselves to a state of celibacy. This state allows them to proclaim the gospel with greater freedom and also to be sign of the kingdom of God which is being ushered in.

Practical significance of celibacy

Celibacy allows such freedom and availability in Christian life and ministry as to make it highly suited to the service of the Church. The priest who is celibate for the sake of the kingdom can carry out particularly difficult missions more easily and freely than a married man, tied down by family responsibilities. The priest can leave for anywhere, at any moment, in response to the Church's urgent request: which the married man cannot do, since he has his wife and children to worry about, their health, their well-being, their education, and all this he has to do if he is faithfully to obey his vocation as a married man.

These human demands, willed by God for the married state, constitute a hindrance to free and available service of the Church. St Paul emphasizes the practical advantage of celibacy inasmuch as marriage entails a necessary loss of independence. "Those who marry will have worldly troubles, and I would spare you that", St Paul writes (1 Cor 7:28). Foreseeing the persecutions to which Christians would fall victim, the Apostle holds that for them it will be an advantage to live in celibacy. The Apostle does not only have the prospect of martyrdom in mind – something hard for a family-man to accept – but the idea too that the married state involves all sorts of worries which distract from the cares of the ministry. Not that celibacy is a tranquil state in which to live far from the cares of the world. The question is merely one of choosing between a life exclusively devoted to the priesthood (and hence, too, to the many anxieties about obedience to Christ, about the mission that has to be discharged and about the community to which one belongs); and a life divided between the two orders of anxiety, that of marriage and that of the Church, both willed by God.

"I want you to be free from anxieties", St Paul goes on. "The unmarried man is anxious about the affairs" of the Lord, how to please the Lord; but the married man is anxious about worldly affairs, how to please his wife, and his interests are divided. And the unmarried woman or girl is anxious about the affairs of the Lord, how to be holy in body and spirit; but the married woman is anxious about worldly affairs, how to please her husband" (1 Cor 7:32-34). The Apostle does not make heavy weather about this division in the hearts of husbands and married women. He does not disapprove of conjugal or family thoughtfulness, but this is an indirect service, whereas celibacy makes it possible to devote all one's time and thought to the direct service of God and the Church.

This was what Christ intended when founding the state of voluntary celibacy "for the sake of the kingdom of Heaven". Establishing a resemblance to Christ which is not only spiritual but physical and practical too, voluntary celibacy is a state particularly suited to the service of the kingdom. Like Jesus, the priest can commit himself entirely – spiritually and humanly – to the ministry. He is not celibate so as to be more tranquil but to resemble Christ in his commitment to the kingdom. If he means to live his state as it should be lived, all his efforts and all his thoughts will have to be directed to a living proclamation of the gospel, so as to hasten Christ's return. He must be ready freely to obey the Church's calls.

The celibate life, which deprives the priest of conjugal

intimacy and fatherhood in the physical order, allows him instead to give himself more completely to looking after other people, to their salvation and to their sanctification. Having no exclusive love, the celibate priest ought always to be at the disposal of all, and he has the time and inner freedom to serve his neighbour (or whoever it be) in charity. It is possible for him to give much time to those who wish to confide in him and he can look after those people who need his sustained support. Furthermore, his being on his own often inspires more trust in those who may wish to confide in him. It is wrong to think he cannot understand people because he does not live as many of them do, with their marital problems and family difficulties. To be guided by the Holy Spirit in directing souls, one need not have experienced every human situation oneself. The priest, being particularly suited to a ministry of spiritual direction, because he is celibate will obtain the hundredfold promised by Christ (Mt 10:29-30). Alhough alone, he will achieve a spiritual fatherhood vis-à-vis those who confide in him willingly.

The inner significance of celibacy

According to St Paul, the unmarried man is not only anxious about the things of the Lord, that is to say, about the ministry to which he can devote all his time, but he is also anxious about how to please the Lord. Similarly, the unmarried woman seeks "to be holy in body and spirit" (1 Cor 8:32-34). "Pleasing the Lord" or seeking "to be holy in body and spirit" should be understood in the mystical sense of a special relationship with Christ, in which prayer and contemplation assume a very important role. Celibacy, as St Ignatius said, is "in honour of the Lord's flesh", it establishes, that is to say, an intimate relationship with the human person of Jesus Christ. The celibate priest has the opportunity of being consecrated directly to Christ in his complete humanity, soul and body. When St Paul reproaches the young widows who had committed themselves to serving the Church, for having gone back on their original pledge of faithfulness to Christ by wanting to get married again, he writes that "the lure of pleasure has distracted them from Christ" (1 Tim 5:11). These words are not to be understood as a moral judgement against marriage as such, but as a reproach addressed to those celibates who, having taken the decision to consecrate their souls and bodies exclusively to the Lord, then go back on the promise they have made. Once we have given ourselves completely to Christ, in honour of his flesh, to be united with him in every aspect of his human nature, to breach this union is an act of infidelity.

Consecrating body and soul to the Lord implies that one wants to please him with all one's life and with all one's being. Every aspect of the celibate priest's life ought therefore to be in accord with making this effort plain. Not only will he seek to live in purity of heart and body, but his behaviour, his words, his relationships, should all reveal the beauty of his vocation.

If the celibate Christian possesses the priestly vocation, the possibility and the privilege of devoting his entire self to the service of other people by giving them all his time and attention, for him the celibate life also means that he must seek to please the Lord in prayer and contemplation. Having chosen the better part, he must do so in such a way that this is not taken from him by the cares of the world. His own celibacy not only signifies what he is, but demands that he be in a state of continual dependence on God. In his loneliness, Christ's love can fill his need for love, and in prayer he will find every joy. Mary's virginity perfectly expresses this sense of total dependency on the Lord. In becoming Christ's mother, Mary did not remain a virgin because marriage was unbecoming to her, but to show that, in giving the world its Saviour, she had consecrated her body and spirit to God alone, in an act of perfect dependence.[4]

The life of prayer and contemplation expressing this

dependence on the Lord assumes a major role in the priest's life. St Paul wanted this for the widows in the early Church, when he wrote to Timothy: "She who is a real widow and is left all alone, has set her hopes on God and continues in supplications and prayers night and day" (1 Tim 5:5). So those who know the loneliness of celibacy are naturally inclined to put their trust in God, to live in unique dependence on and friendship with him and, because of this, will devote part of their time to prayer. Praising the Lord disinterestedly in the Church, the priest will seek means of pleasing him, by honouring him and giving thanks to him in fellowship with the saints. In the Church, the beauty of the liturgy is directly related to this desire to praise the Lord. Liturgical worship expresses love and gratitude for Christ and for his sacrifice. Liturgical prayer and contemplative supplication, freely offered, are not independent of serving the Church and other people, but, by them, in intercession, the priests entrust to the Lord all those for whom they feel they ought to pray. Regular liturgical and contemplative life in the Church, and the Divine Office which the priest is bound to recite even when he is alone, bring him constantly close to Christ in contemplation. St John, the beloved disciple, who more than any of the others was admitted to intimacy with the Lord, gives a perfect description of this attitude of prayerful dependence in the other John, John the Baptist, the first Christian celibate: 'He who has the bride is the bridegroom,' says the Baptist, 'but the friend of the bridegroom, who stands and hears him, rejoices greatly at the bridegroom's voice. Therefore this joy of mine is now full'" (Jn 3:29). Christ had no other bride than the Church, and Christ's disciple has no better friend than the Church's bridegroom. It is enough for him to be close to him and listen to him: the Bridegroom's voice fills him with joy in prayer and contemplation. This dependence as celibate disciple comprises his perfect happiness.

If renunciation of marriage and family is the cause of his loneliness as far as human intimacy goes, the priest should remember there is a promise that corresponds to his commitment. He discovers brothers, sisters and children a hundredfold in time present. Friend of the bridegroom, in the Church he finds the numerous community of all the saints of today and forever. He draws strength and courage from those who, like him, have willed to follow Christ in this special vocation of the celibate life. The priest can no longer think of himself as being alone in the Church and in the fellowship of the saints, since he is the bridegroom's friend and has the opportunity to make himself new brothers by compassion and charity. He is a member of the body of Christ, and all the members of this body are bound together in absolutely indissoluble unity.

In St Paul's invitation to the celibate life, he wishes to bring Christians to a state of nobility and to that which is needed to unite them "without impediments to the Lord" (cf 1 Cor 7:35). These words completely sum up the inner meaning of celibacy. It is an honour, a beautiful and noble condition (*euschemon*). To describe it further, the Apostle uses a word which only occurs once in the New Testament and means a good position near someone (*euparedron*). Through its etymology, this adjective directs our mind straight to the mission of Mary, who sat near Christ so as to hear his word. Celibacy constitutes the better condition for the priestly life. Finally, the adverb which we have translated as "without impediments" (*aperispatos*) once more reminds us of that unique tie to Jesus Christ allowed by the celibate state, and of the loving simplicity that nourishes it.

The eschatological significance of celibacy

Besides the practical and the interior senses which we have described, the state of celibacy also has an eschatological meaning. Voluntary celibacy for the sake of the kingdom of heaven is the sign of a new order in which marriage is no longer, as it was in the Old Testament, necessary to assure a holy progeny to Abraham, the father of all believers. For in the Church, our being children of God and the fellowship of believers are of the spiritual order.

"The time is short", says St Paul, "...the form of this world is passing away." Because of this certainty that the age is coming to an end and that the kingdom is at hand, Christians should have a spirit of detachment with regard to the things of this world. "Therefore let those who have wives live as though they had none, and those who mourn as though they were not mourning, and those who rejoice as though they were not rejoicing, and those who buy as though they had no goods, and those who deal with the world as though they had no dealings with it" (1 Cor 7:29-31). The eschatological sense, the certainty of being at the last act of history and the expectation of Christ's second coming, prompts the Christian not to be too attached to the realities of human life, to marriage, to suffering, to joy or to property. Of course, it is proper to the vocation of the married man to please his wife and concern himself with the things of the world, but he ought to keep reminding himself that the form of this world is passing away. He should not attribute excessive importance to his sorrows and his joys, knowing that in the kingdom of heaven those who now weep will be comforted and that the joy there will be incomparably greater than any experienced here below. Lastly he must be completely convinced that, in the order of the kingdom, the rich will be driven away empty-handed and that the earth belongs to the meek. He should, therefore, live his life undominated by the allurements of the world.

This eschatological attitude should be that of every Christian, but the priest lives it in a more concrete fashion. Among his fellow Christians who all ought to deal with this world without being attached to it, he represents a sign of that detachment which waiting for the kingdom requires. So priestly celibacy does not involve this eschatological sense in an exclusive way, but is a striking sign of the new order which is detached from this world which is passing away.

To the flippant question put by the Sadducees (who did not believe in the resurrection) as to which of her seven successive husbands a woman would find herself married in the after-life, Jesus replied: "The sons of this age marry and are given in marriage; but those who are accounted worthy to attain to that age and to the resurrection from the dead neither marry nor are given in marriage, for they cannot die any more, because they are equal to angels and are sons of God, being sons of the resurrection" (Lk 20:34-36; Mk 12:25; Mt 22:30). Consecrated celibacy is a sign of the resurrection and of the kingdom of God which is drawing near, for in the resurrection and the kingdom there will be neither marrying nor giving in marriage. Celibacy, in the Church, thus draws attention to the new order of the gospel, whereas marriage has its roots in the old order. In the kingdom of God, the fullness of love will be such that no one will feel the need for a limited intimacy any more. On the contrary, it would seem like a diminution of love. So priests are the sign of the fullness of love which will come about in the kingdom.

Furthermore, celibacy relates to the resurrection of the dead; it is a sign of eternity, of incorruptibility, of life. For marriage has as its natural end the procreation of children, it assures the continuance of the human race and the creation of new beings, since human beings are fated to die and need to leave successors. But at the resurrection of the dead, those who have been accounted worthy will no more see death: "They cannot die any more because they are equal to angels and are sons of God, being sons of the resurrection" (Lk 20:36). In the other world, since they are immortal, there is no further need for them to make sure that they have descendants. Besides, in the kingdom of God, there is one sole Father, since all, like the angels, are called sons of God. The celibate state, on account of this relationship with the resurrection of the dead, with eternity and with the angels, is a sign of the world to come, which the priest lives with his whole existence as a follower of Jesus Christ: in the ministry of the gospel, in contemplative prayer at the feet of the Lord, in proclaiming the coming kingdom of God, and in offering the sacrifice of the Eucharist, which sums up his entire priesthood.

NOTES

1. G. Kittel, *Theologisches Wörterbuch zum NT*, t. II, p. 766.
2. K. Barth, *Die kirchliche Dogmatik*, t. III, 6, p. 160.
3. *Letter of Ignatius to Polycarp*, V, W. R. Shoedel, ed. Koester, *Ignatius of Antioch, A commentary on the Letters of St Ignatius of Antioch*, Philadelphia 1985, p. 272.
4. *Maria Madre del Signore, Immagine della Chiesa*, Morcelliana, Brescia 1986, pp. 41-56; L. Legrand, *La virginité dans la Bible*, 'Lectio divina', 39, Le Cerf, Paris 1964, pp. 107-127.

The relevance of priestly celibacy today

Crescenzio Sepe

Titular Archbishop of Grado
Secretary of the Congregation for the Clergy

Conducted by the light of faith, a level-headed analysis of the meaning of terms such as 'relevance', 'modernity' and 'validity' cannot but refer us straight to Jesus Christ, the only paradigm able to verify the basis and truthfulness of what is or is not relevant to the Church of today.

So the problem of the relevance of priestly celibacy cannot evade this 'basic law'. For reference to other criteria would falsify our reasoning and conclusions. Thus, for example, if we wished to refer to purely sociological data or if we thought to interpret the so-called 'signs of the times' as an uncritical survey of socio-cultural conditions present in a given geographical context, then this would not mean anything truly 'relevant', according to the spirit of Christ and of the Church. We have to take the element of grace into account. Celibacy cannot and should not be thought of in a merely negative sense or in reference to the purely natural aspect, according to which it is believed that, once the 'obstacle' or the 'no' to marriage has been removed, a 'boom' in priestly ordinations will be the immediate and natural result. The problem of celibacy comprehends both the natural component, bound up with our sexual nature as the Creator has willed it, and the supernatural component pertaining to the order of grace. Today above all, we tend to emphasize the problems bound up with the first of these elements, simply because hedonism has made us lose certain authentic human values: chastity for example, which is obligatory for all of us whatever our vocation.

And yet, the problems encountered in a correct training for chastity are, from this point of view, the same ones as anyone encounters who aims to attain full maturity of personality. The specific aspects of education, both at seminary and in afterlife, to perfect chastity in priestly celibacy are to be understood not on a merely anthropological terrain but rather on that of grace, in the sphere of which celibacy is not 'the' problem but one among others, and is 'contained' within a symphonic context of priestly training. Human maturation and religious maturation ever go hand in hand and are mutually integrated.

We know that some of those who question the identity and spirituality of the priest in the contemporary world – and celibacy is a very important element of this identity – base their reasoning on evaluations of a sociological kind and hark back to that so-called 'anthropological turning-point', where even the figure of the priesthood is to be 'de-mythologized' or 'de-dogmatized' and the priest, so as to be relevant and a man of his times, temporized and desacralized. In this 'humanizing' design, any reference to the supernatural dimension is seen as 'alienating' by anyone who has not heard of pastoral charity, divine intimacy, tendency to holiness or passion for souls, such as prompted Paul to exclaim: "For to me to live is Christ" (Phil 1:21).

The problem of celibacy is closely connected with that of the ontological identity of the sacrament of Order and with the whole question of the relationship between ordained ministries and instituted ministries, the latter having behind them the amply debated relationship between the universal priesthood of the faithful and the hierarchical priesthood. There exists a substantial interdependence between the sacraments, as a result of which the impoverishment of one has its repercussions on all the rest.

So, for instance, if the Eucharist were to be seen primarily or more or less exclusively as a mere sign of community, Baptism would be conceived of as an initiatory rite without any note of supernaturality, and the priestly ministry would be reduced to a simple function within the community itself. In this way, it would be very hard, if not impossible, to grasp the stupendous connection between priesthood and celibacy, and it would be reasonable enough to think of priests as being *ad tempus*. But would we not gradually come to conceive of an *ad tempus* Christianity as well?

So, if we are to understand the problem of the relevance of priestly celibacy, we must study it within its true dimension: that of the supernatural. To say that priestly celibacy *per se* is not a dogmatic datum must not be taken as meaning that it can be relegated to some 'cultural context' or other. For we have to bear in mind that neither the doctrine nor the life of the Church can be reduced to formally revealed truths and everything else be regarded as arbitrary. On the contrary, these things are to be regarded as the fruit of the guidance and assistance of the Holy Spirit, and part of the Church's two-thousand-year-old tradition.

In the question of celibacy, as in many others concerning the practical life of the Church, we have therefore to avoid minimalism, on the basis of which the only truly legitimate institutions and doctrines would be those of proven apostolic origin or otherwise infallibly defined. Seen aright, it is clear that the Latin discipline of ecclesiastical celibacy is neither arbitrary nor in conflict with the natural right to marriage, even though it cannot be affirmed that it can be deduced from revelation by an irrefutable syllogism. It belongs – indeed, very much so – to the sphere of 'congruity', in the sense that the basis for it lies in the very nature of priesthood.

With these premises in mind, in this essay we shall try to explain what the Christological, ecclesiological and pastoral reasons are which still justify priestly celibacy today, and why those people who tend to call the connection between priesthood and celibacy into question cannot consequently deserve serious consideration.

Christological reasons

The first assertion we still make is that priestly celibacy is relevant *because our Lord Jesus Christ is relevant* who, consecrated Supreme and Eternal Priest by the Father, chose to live his priesthood in chastity and celibacy. We cannot forget, Pope Paul VI states in the encyclical *Sacerdotalis coelibatus,* that the Son of God, who assumed a perfect human nature and raised marriage to the dignity of a sacrament, remained throughout his own earthly life in a state of perfect virginity, to signify his total dedication to the service of God and the human race.[1]

Nor can it be said that the socio-cultural and religious climate in which Jesus lived favoured this kind of life, for we know that in the Jewish environment no condition was so much deprecated as that of a man who had no descendants. Yet Christ willed, harmoniously and intimately, to combine the virginal state with his mission as eternal priest and mediator between heaven and earth. We can therefore affirm that chastity and virginity are not simply additional or secondary to Christ's priestly existence, but belong to its very essence. "Don't you see", St Ambrose writes, "that Christ *is* chastity, Christ *is* integrity?"[2] In becoming priest by virtue of the hypostatic union, the Son of God committed himself to the Father, offering him his total and exclusive love, and consecrated himself entirely to performing the work of redemption.

By priestly ordination, every priest is configured to Christ and shares in his priesthood and, as St Thomas states, *"agit in Persona Christi!"* From this identification with Christ, it follows that he who follows Christ in the priesthood, assents to becoming – in an excellent manner – his witness and to adhering strictly to the ontological connotations of his priesthood.

It is on the strength of this essential, ontological and existential assimilation to Christ that the extreme congruity and relevance of priestly celibacy can and should be judged. The priest, inasmuch as he is an *alter Christus,* finds his true identity, his true *raison d'etre*, his true style, in his intimate, personal relationship with Christ.

The criterion of 'relevance' hence is provided by this essential Christologico-sacerdotal reality and not by passing fashions, mass opinions or certain sociological-type interpretations. If the choices are not faithful to the Model, they are untruthful and false to history: Christ is "the same yesterday and today and forever" (Heb 13:58); so the Christ of 'today' cannot be separated from the Christ of 'yesterday', since he is the Eternal One, the Absolute, and everything refers to him who is 'the' Way, 'the' Truth, 'the' Life.

Like Christ, the priest is called to give himself totally and with undivided heart to God and the brethren, even to the sacrifice of himself. Of course, no one can claim to achieve so exalted an ideal on his own. The call to the priesthood, like celibacy which is linked to it, is a gift which comes from God; it is therefore a supernatural reality, a mystery. "'For not all men', says the Lord, 'can receive this precept, but only those to whom it is given'" (Mt 19:11). Not all, that is to say, are called by God to the height of total self-giving to him in perfect chastity, in accordance with the actual model, Christ. Not to all does God give the potentiality inherent in virginity.

The Second Ecumenical Vatican Council, referring to what is said in St Matthew's Gospel and in the seventh chapter of the First Letter to the Corinthians emphasized that among the various counsels proposed by the Master, there towers up "that precious gift of divine grace given to some by the Father, to devote themselves to God alone more easily with an undivided heart in virginity or celibacy".[3]

To believe in the precious quality of the connection between priesthood and celibacy, to feel its living, joyful relevance, its charm and its riches, one must have faith in God's grace and in his help. In this sense, priestly celibacy "is to be considered as a special grace, as a gift... which does not dispense with, but counts most definitely on, a conscious and free response on the part of the receiver. This charism of the Spirit also brings with it the grace for the receiver to remain faithful to it for all his life and be able to carry out generously and joyfully its concomitant commitments."⁴ The relevance of celibacy is also the relevance of following Christ: "Come, follow me." Following Christ means entering into his mystery of grace and salvation, prolonging his word, his life-style, his sacrificial and saving activity.

This life-style is a transparency of the very life of Christ, the Good Shepherd: "Our priestly life and activity continue the life and activity of Christ himself."⁵ "By virtue of this consecration brought about by the outpouring of the Spirit in the sacrament of Holy Order the spiritual life of the priest is marked, moulded and characterized by the way of thinking and acting proper to Jesus Christ, head and shepherd of the Church and which are summed up in his pastoral charity."⁶

How to follow Christ is set out in the 'evangelical counsels', in imitation of the 'apostolic life': *being* a priest and *acting* as a priest:⁷ being like Christ to act like Christ. This means that, in the Mystical Body, the priest discharges an altogether special task, inasmuch as he has to make the priesthood of Christ the Head sacramentally visible in history. From this, it follows that the figure of the priest is eminently sacramental, whether because, in general terms, he actualizes the mediation of the Incarnate Word, or because he is linked in a unique way to Jesus eucharistically present in his Church. In the eucharistic sacrifice, the priest is not only minister but also part of the sacrificial sign inasmuch as, by offering himself, he signifies Christ.

This virginal relationship with the Body of the Lord, in the sacramental order, is the basis of a formidable and ever relevant congruity as regards the personal chastity of the priest. Eucharist and priesthood must be taken together; because of this, a solid, impassioned eucharistic life in the sacrifice of the cross, love for the Real Presence, zeal for the dignity of eucharistic worship, daily celebration, visits to and adoration of the Blessed Sacrament, constitute elements of exceptional importance for discovering one's own identity and the scope of one's ministry, for permanent character-forming and for pastoral impact.

The force binding celibacy to the priesthood lies in the ontology of the priest. The priestly character, being configured to the priesthood of Christ the Head of the Church, is consequently the instrumental cause conjoined with the supernatural grace in the sacraments, especially in those of the Eucharist and penance. The priest, hence, transmits the divine life to the faithful, and this his supernatural fatherhood must not be confused with or limited to a natural one. His *being* and his *acting* must be like Christ's: undivided.

This is the great teaching bequeathed to us, for instance, by the Apostle of the Gentiles: *"Cor Pauli. Cor Christi!"* exclaims St John Chrysostom. The undivided heart of Paul possessed the splendour of perfect chastity, of celibacy, which he enthusiastically recommended to others when he exclaimed: "I wish that all were as I myself am" (1 Cor 7:7). But the apostolic heart of Paul, precisely because it was undivided, made him fully conformed to that of Christ: perfect chastity in harmony with the other virtues which came to him from assimilation with Christ, made it possible for him to cry: "It is no longer I who live, but Christ who lives in me" (Gal 2:20). Paul: what a relevant example, valid yesterday, today and – yes, indeed – tomorrow.

Ecclesiological reasons

Celibacy is a charism which the Holy Spirit bestows on some in function of a good that redounds to the good of the whole Church. As a charism, celibacy is one of those divine favours which no one can ever dispute, any more than anyone is entitled to dispute the choice made by the Son of God of having an ever virgin Mother and a virgin for his putative father too.

To respect this divine 'favour' and to set the highest value on the 'charismatic' character of celibacy, the Latin Church from earliest times has found it absolutely congruent to unite this gift to the truly sacramental nature of the New Testament priesthood. "The will of the Church finds its ultimate motivation in the link between celibacy and sacred ordination, which configures the priest to Jesus Christ the Head and Spouse of the Church. The Church as the spouse of Jesus Christ wishes to be loved by the priest in the total and exclusive manner in which Jesus Christ her Head and Spouse loved her. Priestly celibacy, then, is the gift of self *in* and *with* the Lord."[8]

Demanding a total and exclusive love, the Church chooses those who, having received the charism of perfect chastity, freely intend to follow the call to continue the mission of salvation bequeathed to them as their heritage by the divine Spouse. And in so doing, the Church is strengthened by the action of the Holy Spirit moving her, through the privileged experience of holiness, to an ever stricter faithfulness to her Lord.

In this sense, the problem of celibacy is not just to be stated at the level of historicity and, therefore, of the out-of-dateness of a 'disciplinary' norm, but on the supernatural plane of Christ's love for his Church. The priesthood is not a gift given for the use of the individual who receives it, but is for others; so, those who receive it have to be able and fit to give themselves totally and unconditionally to the brethren. As Pope Paul VI put it in the encyclical *Sacerdotalis coelibatus*, "The priesthood is a ministry instituted by Christ for the service of his Mystical Body which is the Church. To her belongs the authority to admit to that priesthood those whom she judged qualified – that is, those to whom God has given, along with other signs of an ecclesiastical vocation, the gift of a consecrated celibacy. In virtue of such a gift, confirmed by canon law, the individual is called to respond with free judgement and total dedication, adapting his own mind and outlook to the will of God who calls him. Concretely, this divine calling manifests itself in a given individual with his own definite personality structure which is not at all overpowered by grace."[9]

Hence, ecclesiastical authority will certainly not try to impose a charism on anyone to which he has not been called; but it does have every right to lay its hands exclusively on those who have received the free gift of chastity in the celibate life from the Holy Spirit. The priestly vocation, therefore, is not simply a subjective self-giving on the part of the individual, but requires clear signs of 'vocability' which only the bishop is deputed to ascertain and confirm.

From which it follows that anyone hoping to solve the problem of the shortage of priests (which is grave in certain parts of the world today) along 'democratic' lines, is hopelessly astray: how could a community choose itself a priest and oblige him to live the celibate life and, like Christ, give himself totally to the brethren? For the priestly life, in the context of the Church, is a dedicated life, which implies a limitless gift to the human community, a disposability which is not only deliberate but also effective and affective, to become, in practical terms, a man for all people.

This existential radicalism also illuminates another important ecclesiological reason why celibacy is relevant today: the eschatological dimension. Chastity, above all in its priestly-celibate expression, is a reality which, like charity from which it springs, will last for all eternity. Here below, it is a prophetic sign of that which will be realized definitely in life eternal: a good of the celestial and definitive condition where "they neither marry nor are given in marriage" (Mt 22:30). The Synod Fathers in October 1990 made no bones about it, declaring themselves convinced that "perfect chastity in priestly celibacy... has a prophetic value for the world today", and urgently pressed for "celibacy to be presented and explained... as a precious gift given by God to his Church and as a sign of the kingdom which is not of this world, as a sign of God's love for this world and of the priest's undivided love for God and God's people, so that celibacy be seen as a positive enrichment of the priesthood."[10] This 'proposition' echoes the Apostolic Exhortation *Familiaris consortio,* where it says: "In virginity... the human being is awaiting, also in a bodily way, the eschatological marriage of Christ with the Church, giving himself or herself completely to the Church in the hope that Christ may give him to the Church in the full truth of eternal life."[11]

- In the kingdom of heaven there will be no more marriage! The priesthood of Christ and the whole nature of the Church which springs from him, on this earth already prefigure the eschatological state. To reject the precious link between priesthood and celibacy would be like renouncing that anticipative dimension in the sacramental order of the Church or, at least, very much reducing it. For everyone, believer and non-believer alike, expects a priest not only to be able to speak about the world to come but more important still, to bear witness to it, finding in his chaste and generous way of living an anchor of hope in the difficulties of the present.

So, too, the Apostolic Exhortation *Pastores dabo vobis*[12] takes on and develops this doctrine, which has its most immediate source in the Second Vatican Council, according to which priests with their celibacy "bear witness to the resurrection in a future life"[13] and "they are made a living sign of the world to come, already present through faith and charity – a world in which the children of the resurrection shall neither be married nor take wives."[14]

Priestly celibacy, therefore, is a vigorous affirmation of faith in those supreme values which will one day blaze forth in all the children of God.[15] The priest, prolonging the saving activity of Christ, is in his very being a mystery of that regenerating love for God on which all, no one excluded, can draw. This being so, chastity lived in priestly celibacy is not a frigid refusal to love, much less an alibi for not giving oneself, but on the contrary the charism and perfection of love: the song the priest in company with the whole Church raises to Christ the divine bridegroom during our earthly pilgrimage. Faithful priests will receive the reward from Christ of taking part in the procession of those who "follow the Lamb wherever he goes and sing a new song" (Rev 14:3-4).

Pastoral reasons

The modern world, profoundly secularized and materialistic as it is, constitutes the most exacting challenge for the Church of today. The rich part of the world is going through a process of rationalistic and hedonistic secularization unprecedented in history, alienating human beings from their true origin and their supernatural destiny. The secularist mentality leads, insensibly but inexorably, to behaviour characterized by disregard of the supernatural, uncritical acceptance of a kind of humanism seductive in prospect but ambiguous at its deeper levels, and an unduly touchy preoccupation with one's own self-realization understood as self-centred self-assertion and negation of everything other than self.

In this context, is priestly celibacy still possible and relevant? The question becomes even more alarming if we admit that the mentality described above is dominant not only in the so-called secular world, but can – and often does – infiltrate into the religious and ecclesiastical one as well. The consequences flowing from this are most grave: the tendency to put the work of human redemption before that of the religious and the moral; to make light of the differences between one's own faith and that of the world (and this, not for the praiseworthy effort of seizing on and quickening the environment in which we live, but for trying to assimilate ourselves to it); to prefer the strenuous study of current cultural problems rather than anchor oneself to the sure moorings of revelation and magisterium; to replace the primacy of grace by that of human technology – useful, yes, but only as an instrument.

As we see, the problem of the relevance of priestly celibacy is only one aspect, though a very important and sensitive one, of that more general and fundamental challenge that the Church is facing today and countering with 'the new evangelization'. Anyone who believes and who wishes consistently and realistically to be involved in this urgent task of evangelization, cannot but practise the teaching of the Apostle of the Gentiles: "Do not be conformed to this world" (Rom 12:2). The problems of the contemporary world have to be diagnosed and tackled positively with extreme gospel outspokenness.

To make people aware of the vital relevance of ecclesiastical celibacy, one of the most dynamic elements of evangelization, and we must do all we can to reinvest sacred doctrine with its sapiential atmosphere and metaphysical basis. The world, especially today, has no need of consensus in order to be saved but of transformation and evangelical radicalism, which for every Christian is a fundamental and inalienable requirement, springing from Christ's call to follow him and to imitate him, by virtue of the intimate living fellowship with him, brought about by the Spirit – (cf Mt 8:18ff; 10:37ff; Mk 8:34f, 10:17-21; Lk 9:5ff).

And in truth, even in these troubled times, above and beyond human logic, God does not withhold his many 'wonders'. The Church's history in our day is crystal-clear witness that the Spirit Paraclete is presenting it with "a new era of group endeavours of the lay faithful... movements and new sodalities... with a specific feature and purpose."[16] And indeed, from this new stage in Church history it clearly emerges that pastoral activity in general and priestly activity in particular, if they are to be renewed in response to the demand of the contemporary world, must not follow the policy of giving-in but, on the contrary, that of the Spirit who calls the whole Church community to bear witness to Christ without compromise or reservation.

Proof of this are those same young people of our day who are drawn, not to what is easy, producing instant and temporary results, but to that gospel radicalism which offers the most effective means for living the grandeur of their personal existence and of their dignity as human beings. It would be a grave mistake to think one could attract the young by lowering the gospel peaks to the secularized levels of a world grown materialistic: youth thirsts for great things, for the pure spring in the snowy peaks of the spirit!

"I will give you shepherds after my own heart" (Jer 3:15). "In these words from the prophet Jeremiah, God promises his people that he will never leave them without shepherds to gather them together and guide them..."[17] Convinced of the truth of this, we must urgently construct a pastoral policy for vocations – without delay.

Thus the young will be able to hear, as though in their very ears, the voice of the Lord who from the shores of Lake Tiberias distinctly calls their names summoning them to the most exciting adventure of all of leaving all: to let themselves be filled by the All.

The urgency and intensity with which the Holy Father John Paul II lives the "woe to me if I do not preach the gospel", the missionary zeal with which he infects those fresh energies of the young Churches and rekindles those of the more ancient ones, demand holiness and pastoral fruitfulness from priests above all. This – when one comes to think about it – is only the full actualization of the potentialities inherent in the ontology of priesthood. Seen thus, marriage can be an obstacle to the total priestly devotion needed, inasmuch as it sets up a sphere of legitimate and very intense personal interests, which can be in opposition with the practical demands of the ministry. To put it more clearly, the married state would deprive the priest's life of that precious unity which comes to him, through his various ministerial functions, from his sacramental character.

Immersed in the joys, but in the worries and dangers too, of married life, he runs the risk of becoming purely functional. For only with really great difficulty could the married priest devote – as is his duty – his free time during the day to private prayer and study, these being the necessary aids for living as a man of God. Not overlooking the many and valued examples of married priests of the Oriental Rite, but nonetheless being aware of the general reactions of the people of God, we must ask ourselves whether the priest would still be able to receive the deepest confidence and most heart-felt confessions from people who need to talk to someone whom they feel, at that point in time, to be only and all for them. Would there not be a real risk of his becoming a functionary of the sacraments or a sort of psycho-religious specialist at the mercy of people's subjective needs? For the married priest would be divided between two types of fruitfulness: that of the Church, and that of marriage and bringing up children; and his own heart would bear the sign of division between love for the community and love for his family.

The fact of the matter is that today people living in a cold and lonely society where it is hard to make contact with others need the priest to be available always and no matter how, they need the priest who will be all for God, so as to be all for all. The celibate priest, especially today, is one of the few people, perhaps the last, to be available for others.

The combined problems of vocational pastoral policy, of priestly identity and of life-style most appropriate for priests, are, especially today, a problem of faith. Faith in Christ's providential presence in and assistance to his Church who, if determined to be faithful to the bridegroom, cannot let itself hide or put limits on Christ's countenances. To the world of the young, who have a thirst for the absolute, for prayer and sacrifice, for strong and all-demanding experiences, for exciting missionary incentives, the priest has to present the whole Christ, the Christ of the Cross and Resurrection. The young man who encounters Christ and welcomes his call does not want 'mediations' or 'simplifications'; he consents to follow him with all the strength of his young heart: the celibate life is the logical consequence of his spiritual choice. Since the very beginning, the Church, under the action of the Spirit, has shown her predilection for this spiritual option, with its roots plunging deep into the mystery of Christ the Supreme and Eternal Priest.

How then can we regard as adequately based the reasons of those now trying to loosen or debase the deep link existing between priesthood and the celibate life? It is said, for instance, that the problem of the shortage of priests (a grave one in certain geographical areas today) could be solved if married men were allowed to enter the priesthood. Apart from the fact that this assertion is not supported by either experience or objective data – which rather shows that even where a married priesthood does exist, the problem over candidates for the priesthood has not been solved – one cannot help observing that this proposal does not take sufficient account of the essentially 'catholic' nature of the Church, by reason of which (as has happened in the past), we may hope for an exchange of gifts between those Churches which are particularly rich in priests and those who are short of the same.

The question, furthermore, affects the overall view of the priest and ecclesiastical tradition and cannot be isolated from the many pastoral considerations alluded to above. For this reason, a decision to allow the ordination of married men in the Latin Church could then involve having to take a whole series of interlinked decisions with the knock-on effect of creating stronger pressures for yielding on other points, ending with the abolition of the bond between priesthood and celibacy. We can learn from history here!

Then again, the comparison with the married priests of some Oriental Churches does not seem to be a valid one, for here we have an ancient institution and not one established for reasons of expediency. It must also be said that, actually in those Churches, be they Catholic or Orthodox, the law of celibacy for the priesthood is recommended and held in high regard. This, for example is what a Russian Orthodox bishop of the Patriarchate of Moscow had to say on the subject in the immediate post-conciliar period: "For us Orthodox, the priesthood is a sacred function. For this reason we are convinced that you, Westerners, you Latins, are not on the right path where you allow the question of ecclesiastical celibacy to be debated in public, in the forum of public opinion. In our Oriental tradition, it has been possible to authorize the ordination of a handful of married men, as in any case you have done and go on doing in certain regions. But take care: in the West, *if you separate the priesthood from celibacy, a very swift decadence will set in.* The West is not mystical enough to tolerate the marriage of its clergy without degenerating. The Church of Rome (and this is to her glory) has preserved this ecclesiastical *ascesis* for a whole millennium. Beware of compromising it..."

And a Protestant expresses himself as follows: "This charism of your Church, *consecrated celibacy, has an essential role for ecumenism.* We of the Reformed Churches could certainly do with it too!"[18]

Conclusion

This survey of the factors which constitute the *humus* for an understanding of celibate priesthood, and of those factors which constitute reasons for misunderstanding it, leads to our conclusion about the true relevance of the link between presbyterate and celibacy. For however much we may consider all the arguments against it, none can displace the highest truth.

The 'yes' to celibacy is a question of faith, not only on the part of the men who are ordained, but also on the part of their families and the entire people of God. In the ultimate analysis, we are talking about the folly of the Cross.

Today we find ourselves faced with the pastoral demand for renewal and 'new evangelization'. So be it: the Church will renew itself, as its history of two thousand years attests, but only if it pledges itself to live the gift of itself to Christ its bridegroom with absolute devotion. In these times when conversion is so hard and yet people are easily impressed by others' testimony, the faith needs lives illuminated by the absolute, it needs witnesses who risk their lives, who give their lives away. A sermon of the great Newman comes to mind: "What have you risked for the faith?"

And what more eloquent proof could be offered today to demonstrate that one's own faith is genuine, than that of a free, joyous, warm-hearted renunciation of human love for the sake of Christ and the brethren? The celibate priesthood is one of the strongest responses that can be made to today's pastoral demands, to the new evangelization, to the challenge awaiting the Church in the third millennium. The Lord invites us to put out to sea; if we have faith, fish will abound – for, we know, the Lord sails in the barque of Peter.

NOTES

1. Encyclical Letter of Paul VI (1967), *Sacerdotalis coelibatus*, 21.
2. St Ambrose, *De Virginitate*, 18; PL 16, 271.
3. Dogmatic Constitution, *Lumen gentium*, 42.
4. Post-Synodal Apostolic Exhortation, *Pastores dabo vobis*, 50.
5. *Ibid.*, 18.
6. *Ibid.*, 21.
7. *Ibid.*, 45.
8. *Ibid.*, 29.
9. *Sacerdotalis coelibatus*, 62.
10. Final declaration, *Propositio*, 11, quoted in *Pastores dabo vobis*, 29.
11. Apostolic Exhortation, *Familiaris consortio*, 16.
12. *Pastores dabo vobis*, 29, 50.
13. Decree on the Training of Priests, *Optatam totius*, 10.
14. Decree on the ministry and life of priests, *Presbyterorum ordinis*, 16; cf also *C.J.C.*, cap. I, can. 277.
15. Constitution on the Sacred Liturgy, *Sacrosanctum Concilium*, 34.
16. Post-Synodal Apostolic Exhortation, *Christifideles laici*, 29, 30.
17. *Pastores dabo vobis*, 1.
18. Cf J. Guitton, *Matrimonio e celibato del clero*, in *L'Osservatore Romano*, 22 February 1970, p. 1.

Coeli beatus: Observations of a biologist

Jerôme Lejeune

Pontifical Academy of Sciences

We are the only species on earth to wonder who we are and where we are going, and on occasion to ask ourselves the fearsome questions: "How is it with your brother?"; "What have you done with your child?"

The elementary impulses concerned with perpetuating the species are present in all living beings, but we are the only ones who know about the mysterious relationship between love and the future. Neither the cleverest nor the best trained of chimpanzees could ever conceive there was any relationship between his mounting his female and the arrival nine months later of a baby looking just like him.

We for our part have always known that sexual appetite and its pleasurable satisfaction are by their nature linked to procreation. Didn't the ancients, poetically and absolutely realistically, represent the passion of love with the features of a child?

Human nature

Today all of us know very well that human nature no longer exists. Our impulses and actions, especially in the sexual sphere, are no more than mere conventions imposed by society and varying according to the times. As the neo-humanists have now formally decreed, there is no biological law to guide or enlighten us.

Given that the scientific spirit does not accept sweeping statements without benefit of supporting evidence, we may be permitted to think twice before accepting that the instincts of our species do not exist or that the amorous impulses are only meaningless, illogical tremors. Neuro-anatomy shows us how rash it would be to disregard how we are made. The 'skin sack' which covers and defines this house of flesh in which we dwell is replicated point by point in the cerebral cortex. At about the height of the head-band which girls sometimes use to keep their hair in place, on the posterior slope of the fissure of Rolando, a sensory representation of our entire body may be observed.

The neurological homunculus[1] is as it were stretched out on the ascending parietal, its head turned downwards, the legs upwards, with the feet dangling in the furrow separating the two hemispheres. The parts are all to be found in the normal order: head, neck, hand, arm, trunk, pelvis, leg, foot and toes and, below the toes, the genital organs. This arrangement, surprising at first sight, is abso-lutely logical once we remember we walk upright. If we went on all fours, we should see that the genital organ would be in effect at the posterior extremity of the trunk and would consequently be projected immediately after the representation of the leg and toes.

Thus the genital sphere is the only part of our body, the cerebral representation of which comes into direct contact with the enormous limbic lobe, the seat of all the emotions. For it is in this last that the impulses are organized that move us: those which have to do with the survival of the individual (hunger, thirst, aggression) and those concerned with the continuation of the species (genital appetite, at-traction to a partner, protection of the young, loyalty to one's own kind).

From this it follows that we are so made that what involves the sphere directly disturbs morality from a neurological point of view. Hence the impossibility (it would seem) of curbing emotional behaviour and control-ling the instincts, if the empire of the will does not extend to, and perhaps especially to, conscious and deliberate genital behaviour.

The old witticism of the cynical in days gone by, "If

morality exists, it's a pity it's sited in one's pants", only showed ignorance of neuro-anatomy. The rigorists were certainly not mistaken in siting the genital organ in close contact with the emotions: it was memory of life.

Fontes vitae

From time to time all through life, the amorous impulses make themselves felt, whether in isolation or all at once, and it is the individual's job to hold them in balance. Being a particularly powerful impulse, *the genital appetite* can manifest itself in complete isolation in the lowest orders of living creatures. Certain male fish, for instance, scatter their sperm over eggs laid by a female they do not know and will never meet. If reduced to the genital impulse, sexual behaviour would be satisfied with a mere automatic discharge.

In higher creatures, *attraction to the opposite sex* directs this appetite and, in us, tenderness completes its meaning: the union of two people is needed to generate a third. This typical trilogy of natural reproduction[2] requires that affection unite persons of differing sex. Whence the expression in common usage, regarding the homosexual relationship as against nature in that it satisfies the appetite in a counterfeit way[3] and can in no way respect the partner, much less the child.

The transmission of life is not exhausted in procreation: the protection of the young represents the obligatory sequel to it. This impulse is so strong in all vertebrates (and even in invertebrates), there seems a need to insist on its importance for us human beings. At the newborn child's first cry, anyone can feel the tug of this irresistible call. Abortion and infanticide,[4] however, show how terribly human nature can be distorted.

Lastly, loyalty to the family and the group, this feeling of belonging, this need to give oneself totally, comprises the basis of society. The abandoning of babies, however, or doing away with the sick (as certain trend-setters, tirelessly dusting off the most ancient sophisms, recommend) show how vulnerable these instincts are in our species.[5]

The natural sciences, however, are in no position to take us any further. While not abandoning hope of a deeper analysis, the biologist prudently and respectfully observes this exquisitely human phenomenon of the commitment of persons:

– leaving father and mother in order to form one flesh forever with a spouse of one's own may be easy to imagine;

– protecting one's children, parents and all members of one's group seems just what one should hope for;

– giving up one's life for those whom one loves, this too is conceivable, at least in theory.

Without pretending to ignore the difficulties and sufferings or simply the inconveniences of marriage, it is obvious it gives equilibrium to loving relationships. So why reject the humble joys of the hearth, the charm of children, the warmth of family and group? Why this voluntary forsaking of these guaranteed forms of happiness? No inclination predisposes us in this direction. This notwithstanding, consecrated celibacy clearly shows that another kind of equilibrium is possible.

Coelibatus

The thought processes of a biologist cannot hope to explain a religious phenomenon; they are, however, able to study its more obvious effects. The feeling of belonging can find its highest form of development in celibacy. These words of an experienced missionary bear witness to the fact. "In all my career," he said, "and in the most god-forsaken places, I have never encountered strangers. Wherever I've been, I've found brothers and sisters."

For seen from heaven, if one may use such an expression, the view is wider. The priest recognizes one of his

86

own kind in his neighbour, but at the same time feels, in the brother or sister, he sees the spirit of the Father, whom he does not see. Human nature is a distorting mirror, scratched and blistered by the scar of our original sin, our intellect divided between reason and heart. But this uncertain likeness, this indistinct image, almost unrecognizable indeed, can nonetheless be perceived by him whose eye is changed.

Protection of the little ones can also be exercised to the full. A brilliant Christian intuition has been to associate the virtue of goodness to the parental character.

Women who serve the poorest, the marginalized, the little loved, are rightly known as 'sisters' and more rightly still as 'good'. More than any sociological or statistical parameter, the role of the *good sisters* is the empirical measure of the degree of Christianity. A detail of dress is helpful to them in their work. The veil is extremely useful in that it prevents the affection shown and the charity lavished from being subjected to false interpretations. A little sister of the infirm observed that, dressed as well as possible, as is the case today, she no longer dared to enter shady neighbourhoods with the same confidence as before. "The people", she said, "can no longer tell in whose name I am coming." This was how she expressed her personal commitment: the sole reason for celibacy. And this is how a superior gave me to understand it, as she guided her convent with most effective sweetness: "*Commitment, choosing the bridegroom,* yes, we're talking about vocation. It is said that priests and nuns must not get married, so as to be fully available to consecrate themselves to God and devote themselves to other people.

– Of course, this is perfectly true, but the truth lies the other way around: when one is fully committed to God, how can one contract a *second* marriage?

– To our postulants, I answer: If you don't feel called to follow the Lord as one of his companions, go and find yourself a husband. Both vocations are OK, but not both at once!"

This leaves *the genital appetite,* our most insistent and

explosive of impulses, at least on the physical level. However fundamental it may be (and on it depends the future of the species), this biological function is the only one that does not produce a pathological condition if left unsatisfied. One cannot say the same for hunger, thirst or the need for sleep.

In celibacy the impulse persists, always just as specialized, yet the appetite gradually becomes generalized. From having been genital, it grows ingeniously back up the tree of life to him who begat it. By seeking our happiness on the other slope of time, the human being, healed at last, is united to the infinite Present.

This appetite for the sublime is perhaps the origin of the word *coelibatus*. Seneca used it for the unmarried state. Julius Valerianus applied it to the life celestial. This little known historian had perhaps come closer to the truth than distinguished moralists: the heart that renounces earthly loves for the greatest love of all is indeed *Coeli beatus*.

NOTES

1. More accurately, one ought to speak of the semi-homunculus, given that the right side is projected on the left side of the brain and vice-versa, and the human figure is upside down and set cross-wise. Another detail: the head is separated from the trunk, as though held between the fingers. The neuronal man, in effect, does not have a head on his shoulders. Here too, typology unveils the mystery: this arrangement permits the simplest possible wiring system to project on a flat surface each point of a sphere linked with a cylinder, the head mounted on the neck.
2. This is to say: when the conjunction of the gametes is the result of the union of the persons and not of the act of a third agent, as in the case of *in vitro* fertilization or of artificial insemination by syringe.
3. Our own age knows all too well what devastation has been wrought by sodomy. The AIDS epidemic is a fearful example of this. We are not talking in terms of a punishment, of course, but merely of the result of acting against nature. God alone can forgive those who break his laws; human beings forgive only rarely; nature never does, not being a person.
4. Abortion and infanticide are abominable crimes (Vatican II, *Gaudium et spes*, 51).
5. For each of these cases, analogies may be found throughout the animal kingdom. Among the higher animals, one may cite examples which, although isolated, are extremely striking, and which are indeed pretty instructive, for all that the mechanism that triggers them off is unconscious.

Priestly celibacy in the light of medicine and psychology

Wanda Poltawska

Professor of Pastoral Medicine at the Pontifical Academy of Cracow

Unlike celibacy for lay people, the celibacy of the priest is determined by the free and conscious choice made by a psychically mature man (it is one of the main conditions put to anyone wishing to take Holy Orders) and as such does not cause a sense of frustration. This however is a very common psychological reaction among single lay people who would like to get married but cannot, and so feel 'condemned' to a life of loneliness. Reactions of this sort are more common in women than in men, and in many cases the ungratified desire for married life and motherhood gives rise to bouts of psychic depression.

Making a choice always means giving up other possibilities, other values, but a free choice willingly made also bears witness to the conviction that the value chosen is superior to all the other ones. The priesthood is so charged with potential for self-realization as to give the life of the man who has chosen it a sense of fullness which is often lacking in the lives of ordinary people. Spiritual fatherhood, the power to bind and loose, the joy of bearing, with his own hands, the supreme gift of God himself to others: these place the priestly dignity on so high a plane in the hierarchy of human possibilities that it cannot be compared with anything else what-so-ever and leaves no room for frustration.

As most people see it, the priest is bound forever to the obligation of celibacy and, generally speaking, this disposition of the Church has hardly been challenged in past centuries. The vocation to the priesthood and the vocation to marriage both require the same total devotion and hence are mutually exclusive, even though the type of personality required is basically the same in both cases. In the twentieth century, however, we do not so much have a repudiation of the actual ideal of celibacy as doubt over the real possibility of sticking to decisions connected with it.

When John Paul II speaks of priestly celibacy, he often qualifies it as 'sacred' – 'sacred priestly celibacy' – emphasizing that it is not just a matter of renouncing married life, for its deep significance lies in chastity and virginity, in supreme union with God.

Celibacy and the sixth commandment

Because of the growing tendency to permissiveness and the exaltation of the biological dimension of human nature, the modern world tends to deny people's ability to live chastely throughout their lives. By some people, the renunciation of sexual activity is perceived as a punishment, by others as an unattainable ideal, by yet others as a way of life which is 'against human nature'.

Forgetting the special grace of the sacrament which affords the support and strength needed for fulfilling such a vocation, people often confuse priestly celibacy with the celibacy of lay people who, having no deep motivation, do not keep the sixth commandment, even though considering themselves believing Catholics. The law laid down by God and intended for everyone "not to fornicate", they also question on the basis of what they see going on every day around them. So many people transgress this commandment today that it might well seem 'unsuited' to human capacities, as though it were impossible to observe it.

This increasingly widespread permissive ethics has given rise to an attitude of expectation of a definite change in the teaching of the Church, not only over priestly celibacy but indeed over all standards and, among others, over the obligations of the sixth commandment. Seeking from purely pastoral motives to help the people of today, whose specific life-style is largely governed by conceptions of comfort, the Church has already relaxed certain rules of conduct, and this has aroused expectation of further changes, especially in questions, the definition of which pertains to the ecclesiastical authorities and is not directly derived from divine revelation.

Since priestly celibacy, introduced on the basis of experience, has intrinsically the nature of human and not divine decision, the people of the twentieth century seem to be waiting for 'something to change'. This attitude of uncertainty, of the 'open door', makes respect for chastity even harder, even on the part of priests. Now, the final and unequivocal decision – "I choose celibacy once and forever, beyond all hope of recall" – like all unequivocal and final decisions, is easier to fulfil than an uncertain one – "Perhaps I will, but we'll see about that – later" which encourages the sin of fornication by weakening the mechanism of self-control needed for keeping the sixth commandment. There is a fairly general conviction that the only cure for the problems connected with celibacy would be to allow the clergy to get married. For the frequency with which fornication is committed raises doubts over the real possibility of living according to other models. Modern people often forget that the sixth commandment applies to everyone without exception, and that no circumstances exist that can suspend the validity of this divine law.

The question next arises whether the abolition of celibacy should just constitute permission to contract indissoluble marriage, or rather lead to a demand for the introduction of the right to a sex life independent of marriage, that is to say, basically, an attempt to sanction fornication in general, and even for priests. The growing tendency to recognize the 'rights' of the young to sexual activity often means that preparation for the sacrament of marriage, as also for the priesthood, will have been preceded by 'pre-sacramental' fornication, whether of hetero- or homosexual type. Experiences of this sort, to some degree, condition the behaviour of the person and leave an imprint, a memory, which will later make control of the individual's own reactions even harder.

The false conception of sexuality

The permissive sexual ethics of today originates in a false conception of human sexuality in general. The fact of being endowed with sex, which makes human reproduction possible, does not make the sex act necessary *per se*. We are not programmed as to our sexual activity; in the human organism there exist no mechanisms forcing us to act in this way. The only thing determined is sexuality, the Creator's gift, transmitted by our parents at our first instant of life. The whole somatic structure and psychic development of the human being are closely connected with sex as they develop; human existence, in every one of its aspects, bears the features of sexuality; everything we achieve in the course of our lives is marked by it. Hence, sexuality is a way of existing in the world and it is, therefore, absolutely wrong to speak of it as something separate from the human entity: sex as such, as an abstract concept separate from us, does not exist. Only the human being exists, endowed with sexuality: unable to shed our own sexuality, we are male or female, as the case may be, throughout our lives. The whole human body bears the features of this innate sexuality and is subject to a complex nervous system and biological functions which are independent of our will. The human organism, the supreme work of the Creator, is in its complexity a very harmonious whole, ordered with a fascinating precision independent of the subject. Without being commanded by the human will, the body of its own accord follows the laws of its own nature: all the reactions occurring in the organism in the course of its entire life-cycle come from God and are his gift.

Endowed with all the organs needed for living, the

human body also possesses those, improperly called sexual, which are however essentially procreative, their function being to pass on the gift of life. By endowing us with these organs, the Creator has granted us the opportunity of collaborating with him in the great work of creation.

In collaboration of this sort, the human person is called by God to the sacrament of marriage, which unites husband and wife in accordance with the divine plan – "they will be two persons in a single body" – on which the physiological structure of the human organism depends. But not all of us are called to be parents: some of us have other tasks to discharge. The call to reproduce, even though frequent, is not common to all. Sexuality, as a characteristic of the individual, is given to each of us; but procreation is the task only for those who have been called to it by the Creator.

The myth of orgasm

The sexual act uniting husband and wife needs some stimulus to the sexual organs, for these normally remain inactive. A person with normal reactions does not feel any particular excitement of a sexual nature unless it is induced. The concept of sexual instinct, with reference to human beings, is therefore rather imprecise: in the literal sense of the term, such an instinct does not exist; only certain sexual reactions exist that the human being can go along with but can also control and curb. To be performed, the sex act needs an initial state of excitement, as is easily observed, especially in the male organism. This excitement, which may be caused by an impulse of physiological, emotional or volitional type, is not only easy to achieve but is also perceived as a pleasurable sensation. The culminating point, known as orgasm, is only the final mechanism for effecting procreation. It makes fertilization easier, even though, obviously, it does not determine it. But orgasm, being a particularly intense and deeply-felt sensation, often becomes the only objective; it becomes divorced, that is to say, from its reproductive function, all the more so since it is considered to be a 'sign' of the love with which the actual sex act is often mistakenly identified.

People today yearn for pleasure and look for it wherever they can. Modern sexology gives precise descriptions of different methods for achieving orgasm and of the techniques for causing it, often overlooking the fact that this state of maximum excitement is only a means and not an end, and that it can give rise to conception and all the problems associated with the role of parenthood. The hedonistic attitude puts orgasm among the most desired objectives at which human beings can aim. By the sheer fact of being endowed with sex, human beings feel somehow authorized to be sexually active, sometimes even claiming to be forced to be so by their own somatic reactions. In this way, human beings come to be dominated by their physiological mechanisms.

Mistaken concept of virility

The ease with which it is possible to stimulate sexual excitement encourages many people to search for pleasure and the subsequent easing of tension. But this sort of excitement, above all when not determined by the will, is quite easily curbed by the will. For what differentiates us human beings from the animals is our ability to control our own reactions. The secretion of the gametes is independent of the human will; sexual activity, however, is always a result of the free decision of the individual. Often people not only say 'I want' but also 'I ought to do it', and this 'I ought' is not a real physiological necessity, but only a reinforcing of 'I want'. But if the mere permissive attitude, 'I want', is already enough to stimulate excitement, the prohibition, 'I mustn't', is not enough to curb the reaction. And here lies the most difficult problem: prohibition is not only of little use but in many cases produces the opposite effect; by releasing the transgressive mechanisms, it increases the excitement. Thus boys who try to give up masturbating often make the mistake of repeating over and over to themselves the prohibition, "mustn't do it because it is a sin". Simple prohibition thus is not the right approach, since it creates further tension and is hard to put into practice; what is important though is the conscious free choice: "I do not commit the sin, not because it is forbidden to do so but because I am conscious of the fact that it is wrong and give it up of my own free will."

Identical considerations hold true for priestly celibacy: if the candidate for the priesthood is not deeply motivated in making his choice and renouncing matrimony, he will never appreciate the value of chastity and totally immerse himself in God's love.

Celibacy as a life-style

In choosing a way of life, a man who is psychologically mature ought to be quite clear too about the way his decision will work out in practice and be aware of the results and of the responsibilities involved. Many factors contribute in differing degrees to psychological and emotional maturity, but above all the repeated and constant work one does on oneself. As complex entities, we have the task of realizing our capacities, but only by uninterrupted effort can we reach that degree of maturity which Karol Wojtyla calls 'self-possession' (cf *The Acting Person*, London 1979), which is indispensable for the realizing of any vocation.

Priesthood precludes marriage not so much because the Church has decided that it does, but rather because, requiring an absolute devotion, it leaves no room for the commitment, equally total, demanded by marriage and fatherhood. Unfortunately, the future priest often lives in an environment where the hedonistic attitude prevails and hence the ideal of total devotion is not respected.

Asceticism in the Christian's life

In today's world, believers often do not manage rationally to grasp the deeper sense of Christianity. Loving our neighbour involves a need for renunciation, helping the person loved sometimes requires a real sacrifice. Life in Christ demands a constant availability to sacrifice, all the more so the life of someone proposing to enter Holy Orders.

Of the various values one is called upon to renounce in order to become a priest, there is also the possibility of exercising one's own sexuality. But since it is commonly thought that sexual activity is to be identified only with pleasure, the requirement of celibacy is seen as deprivation of that pleasure. From the point of view of the physiology of the human body, the renunciation of sexual activity does not mean the mortification of any one particular demand, since the body does not possess mechanisms constraining it to act in this way. The male genital organs, the constant activity of the gonads as endocrine glands notwithstanding, do not react without being stimulated. Chastity thus does not exert any negative effect on the organism; indeed one might say there is a saving of energy, permitting the subject to concentrate his attention on other activities.

Now, to reach such a state of harmonious equilibrium, and beyond a decisive attitude of will, one needs to live an ordered life, maintaining a certain physical and psychic 'hygiene' and inner discipline. It is also necessary to understand how one's body works, to know its reactions and the mechanisms that trigger these off. By knowing the way one's body reacts, one can avoid the stimuli that provoke unwanted reactions, since our body is obedient to our will, if we learn how to control it. The somatic reactions are always conditioned by an external impulse and hence, as it is possible to make it more sensitive to external stimuli, so it is also possible to control it in such a way that it does not respond to such stimuli. The boy, as he matures, learns to understand the mechanism of his own reactions and how to control them.

In practice, we are all obliged to acquire this ability to control our own reactions since the very demands of social life compel us to do so. For the sexual act, belonging as it does to the most intimate sphere of our entity, never takes place spontaneously under the impulse of the moment, but always has to have a context and a right moment; and this involves the necessity of controlling the somatic reactions. Spontaneity in the literal sense of the word does not exist in human sexual activity.

Now, the priest, by virtue of the vocation he has chosen, has to be aware that for him the possibility of activating the mechanisms of sexual reaction does not exist and that, by activating them, he comes into collision with himself and the vow he has pronounced. From situations of this sort, neuroses can arise: it is not celibacy that creates the stress but the lack of firmness in carrying it out on account of psychical immaturity, simple human weakness or insufficient acceptance of the ideal of celibacy itself.

On the other hand, if the candidate for the priesthood learns to avoid the stimuli and if he looks on other people as one big family, as Jesus teaches, he will not mind abstinence particularly, nor will he yearn for a different life-style, since the one he has chosen makes him happy and fulfilled.

Maturity and religious realism

In the process of maturing physically and mentally, we each become aware of the purpose of our own existence and of the meaning of life as such. For the believer, maturity means being aware of the limitations of earthly life, and the eternity of life in God. The prospect of eternity helps us patiently to endure the hardships that may turn up in life, thanks to our being aware that they are only fleeting. The priest's job is not only to point out the true dimension of human existence to believers, but also to bear witness to it in his own life. The words of Jesus on the Last

Judgement have particular relevance for those individuals to whom 'more has been given'. The priest, by his nature, represents the apogee of human potentiality: no higher dignity exists, nor greater responsibility.

Now, awareness of responsibility, which God's gift entails, constrains us to reflect deeply. The gift of sexuality is not simply a gift but, like all life, is also a task laid before us. Chastity does not in fact constitute an absence of positive experience but, on the contrary, through the effort of the will, a means of reaching a state of equilibrium, an inexhaustible sense of satisfaction and joy. The sex act offers only a second of pleasure and often leaves a feeling of shame and embarrassment as regards one's own reactions. The knowledge of having full power over one's own instinctual reactions, however, gives one not only real joy but above all a feeling of freedom, since only at the time when we become capable of living in conformity to the chosen system of values can we say that we are truly free. The happiness that comes from this is pure and lasting, and it helps us to achieve a state of psychic equilibrium.

People who manage to realize these principles in daily life radiate their own inner peace and harmony to others. The influence that priests endowed with this particular ability exert on other people is enormous, since the need for peace is common to all. Sin always makes for anxiety; virtue, even if dearly purchased, brings joy. Besides awareness of the grace of which he is trustee, the privilege of offering God to others in the sacraments ought to fill the priest with still greater joy and gratitude for his vocation. In such a situation, celibacy cannot constitute a real hardship, since he is so filled with grace and divine love as to forget all about himelf, as the lives of many a holy priest bear witness.

Difficulties in observing celibacy

Today's way of thinking presents an obstacle to the ideal of priesthood as the quest for personal sanctity and the sanctification of the world. The difficulties the priest encounters in following his vocation are of various kinds, but those connected with the observance of celibacy are particularly grave, since transgressing this obligation usually means sinning against the sixth commandment. A religious, in point of fact, never asks for a dispensation and permission to get married before having committed the sin. But it cannot be forgotten that in the life of the priest there no longer exists a power of choosing between priesthood and marriage: the choice has already been taken and is to all intents and purposes irrevocable, for reneging on one's own commitment signifies moral degradation.

(a) *Mistaken concept of sexuality*. Difficulties are likely to arise once the priest gives in to the widely held view that human beings are biologically determined. The erroneous notion that the male is in a sense compelled to sexual activity by virtue of the very fact of being male, is becoming stronger and stronger. People even think that the sexual act 'proves' one's virility; that without it, a man is in some way disabled, unrealized. Concepts of this sort, especially if repeated by medical authorities in the sexological field (as often happens) can easily be used to justify one's own behaviour. From now on the individual, dominated by his own body, justifies himself by saying that 'it is not possible' to act otherwise.

(b) The other factor that makes curbing one's sexuality more difficult is *physical* and *psychical exhaustion*, accompanied by an excess of stimuli, especially visual ones. People react particularly intensely to visual impressions, and Jesus himself warns us against the temptations of the eye. If images of an erotic kind are added to stress, increased by the abuse of nicotine, caffeine and the like, the mechanism of self-control may be weakened, especially in the young.

Chastity requires a constant discipline and a constant hygiene in one's life-style. By giving way to the stimulus, we cannot expect the body to be able to resist the somatic reactions easily; the body on its own does not have the ability to control its own reactions. Stimuli which may cause sexual reactions are of various kinds. The simplest sort, the mechanical ones for instance, are generally easy to avoid, and even very young boys are usually able to curb them. More dangerous, however, are those which come from within us, from the imagination.

So it is extremely important for every priest to know how to maintain discipline over his thoughts and his imagination. For one can also sin alone, in thought: by looking at another person with desire, by treating that other person as an object, the sin of fornication is committed in the depths of the heart. If an attitude of this sort dominates the heart, it will also manifest itself outside. On the other hand, if we are clean within, no external situation can provoke somatic reactions against our will. Sexual excitement depends, in the first place, on the intentions with which we approach our neighbour, how we look at him or her and what we see there. The priest is obliged to see the very Christ in his neighbour; the aim of any encounter can only be to bring that person nearer to God.

The entire human body shares in the specific vocation of each individual, for without a physical structure we cannot exist. So the body too has to help the priest in his task as the shepherd of souls. Maturity brings the father's role, particularly to the priest, whose task it is to beget souls (see St Paul).

Lust tends to subordinate others to our will, subjugating them and humiliating them by treating them as objects. A father's love, however, offers itself, asking nothing in return. But to attain to this, one must teach the body self-control. Chastity is, therefore, a constant effort to subject the body entirely to the aspirations of the soul. Each human being's body is always subject to a spirit: either to the Holy Spirit, or to the spirit 'of this world'.

(c) *The weight of the past.* Not without reason, in days gone by, did the Church demand virginity of candidates for the priesthood, for one of the conditions making the observance of celibacy especially hard is the memory the body retains of its own past experiences. Return to God and renewal of the soul are always possible but, since the body retains the memory of the past, even if the sin has been absolved, its effects persist. Being used to surrendering to a given type of reaction, the body finds it hard to submit to a new kind of discipline; as a result, those who have committed the sins of fornication or masturbation find the obligation of celibacy all the more difficult to observe. The same is true for pornographic pictures: the memory retained by the eye, if on the one hand it makes the whole sexual sector seem hateful, on the other provokes excitement and internal conflict. Obviously the priest cannot be isolated from the world around him; the important thing is to protect that great gift of his chastity. Important to this end will be inner discipline, but more important still the capacity for admiring the beauty radiated by innocence and chastity.

(d) *Lack of faith.* When we analyze the lives of those priests who have not managed to keep the obligaction of celibacy, one cause stands out as common to almost all of them: moral degradation. Usually this sets in with a crisis of faith and a rejection of the rules laid down by the Church, that is to say, in the ultimate analysis with a lack of humility. Usually, the law of celibacy is broken by men who are too sure of themselves, who do not seek the support of divine love. Holiness, although it requires the individual's collaboration, is primarily the gift of divine grace, a gift that needs to be humbly asked for in prayer. When the passion for prayer grows cool, the priest more easily becomes a prey to the pressures of his environment.

Celibacy, as an attempt to overcome oneself and one's own frailty, is a going 'against the current', is a challenge hurled at the world, but it is never a going against human nature. For, by the very fact of being human beings, we are able to control our own reactions, since we are not to be identified solely with our bodies: we are souls embodied, created by God and created in his likeness. The demand of celibacy does not exceed human capacities: Christ himself shows us the way when he bids us to seek perfection.

The conscious quest for holiness is not against the individual, but against our individual paltriness and leads us to transcend ourselves. A full realization of priesthood and celibacy develops the human personality to its full potential and hence makes it easier to achieve the objective to which we all are summoned – holiness.

Priestly celibacy and problems of inculturation

Polycarp Pengo

Archbishop of Dar-es-Salaam (Tanzania)

Celibacy in the form demanded of the Roman Catholic priest, namely, a life-long abstinence from marriage, is probably foreign to all human cultures. No wonder, therefore, that priestly celibacy causes everywhere a number of problems in the question of inculturation of the faith. In the light of the post-synodal Apostolic Exhortation *Pastores dabo vobis* of the Holy Father Pope John Paul II, I wish to make a brief study of some of those problems hoping thereby to point out some direction in which to look for the solution to some of those problems.

In number 50 of the above mentioned post-synodal Exhortation we read the following profound words:

> Priestly celibacy should not be considered just as a legal norm, or as a totally external condition for admission to ordination, but rather as a value that is profoundly connected with ordination, whereby a man takes on the likeness of Jesus Christ... as a choice of a greater and undivided love for Christ and his Church.

For Tanzania, at least, I believe that priestly celibacy presents seemingly insurmountable problems for the inculturation of the Christian faith because this papal message has not been properly grasped and appreciated.

As a preliminary note I wish to express that, according to me, true and authentic inculturation is a form of 'Incarnation', meaning, introducing the spiritual, divine reality into a body, a tangible and comprehensible reality so that the spiritual or the divine can become tangible and compre-

103

hensible. Therefore, the predominant factor or element in the concept of inculturation is the divine or the spiritual. This is the primary concern and the ultimate goal in the entire process. In other words, the divine spiritual element must take precedence over the human, material reality or aspect in every task of inculturation.

In the above quotation of the Holy Father, an intrinsic connection is made between the notion of priestly celibacy and the very person of Christ: celibacy is *not just a legal norm* (a human affair) but the *likeness of Jesus Christ*. There is no doubt that in the priestly celibacy of the Catholic Church there is also an element of 'legal norm' and of 'external condition'. That element needs to be taken into consideration to the extent that it contains some human value or, I would even say, a cultural value. But such a human or cultural value cannot be the ultimate criterion for inculturation. It has to be weighed and evaluated against other human or cultural values for its determinative value in realizing inculturation.

Priestly celibacy as a purely human or cultural value

a. Priestly celibacy viewed from the economic point of view

There are quite a number of similarities between the priesthood in the Old Testament and the priesthood of the New Testament continued and developed in the Christian religion. One of the points of similarity is the lack of property for inheritance. Priests in the Old Testament had no land apportioned to them which they could bequeath to their descendants. The Lord was the portion of their inheritance, and so they lived out of the offerings presented to the Lord.

Similarly, priests in the New Testament have no property of their own which they might leave for their children to inherit. They live entirely dependent on the offerings of the community of believers and on the property of the entire Church. Thus, in both the Old and the New Testament, the priest depends entirely on Church possessions for his living.

Besides the points of similarity between the two priesthoods, there are other points of considerable differences. One of these is the way the priesthood is transmitted. In the Old Covenant, no one could become a priest unless one was descended from the tribe of Levi. That meant, priesthood itself was inherited together with the economic assurance of living from the altar of the Lord. Even those descendants of Levi who for one reason or another could not exercise their priestly ministry still maintained the right to live from the altar of the Lord (cf Lev 21:16-23).

On the other hand, the priesthood of the New Covenant is single and perfectly realized in the one High Priest, Jesus Christ, who himself neither inherited his priesthood from Aaron or any Levite nor could he pass his priesthood to anyone else as an inheritance. He lives for ever and so he cannot be inherited; this being one of the main ideas in comparing Christ's priesthood to that of Melchizedek in the Letter to the Hebrews (cf chapter 7).

Every priest in the New Testament simply participates in that priesthood of Christ; the priesthood he cannot pass on to his descendants. Thus while the children of the Old Testament priests were assured of their livelihood through the inheritance of the priesthood itself, those of the New Testament would either have to provide for their future without any assistance from their father or they would have to divide up Church possessions among themselves.

Already in the sixth century, Emperor Justinian realized the danger of the property of the Church being alienated through the inheritance of priests' children who were themselves not priests. Thus he issued decrees which were the first steps towards obligatory celibate priesthood. He demanded that "a person who had children could not be a bishop, and a married cleric must live with his wife as with a sister" (cf J.M. Ford, 'Celibacy' in *A New Dictionary of*

Christian Theology). In fact, Emperor Justinian was continuing, perhaps in a more diplomatic way, the efforts already visible during the Council of Nicaea (AD 325) to try to make celibacy obligatory among clerics.

The Gregorian reforms in the eleventh century on this question of priestly celibacy can also be partly understood in the same economic perspective. The reforms were intended not only to encourage the semi-monastic standard and spirit among the clergy but also, and probably mainly, to prevent priests from being too absorbed in the feudal system with its central concern of material possessions.

There is no doubt that the question of material possession and the economic well-being of priests has always played some role in the maintenance of the institution of priestly celibacy in the Catholic Church. It is not rare in our ecumenical dealings with the Protestant brothers to hear them speak approvingly of the Catholic Church's maintenance of priestly celibacy. And their main reason for this is that priestly celibacy enables an economically better state for the Roman Catholic priest.

However, the economic aspect of priestly celibacy cannot be taken as the sole or even as the main reason for maintaining priestly celibacy. First of all, this reasoning as a basic attitude of mind expresses a rather selfish spirit in the priest. Moreover, such a reason alone would easily lead to infidelity which goes together with the alarmingly increased involvement of clerics in economic enterprises.

Coming to Tanzanian culture, the economic question would be even less of a reason for maintaining priestly celibacy. In the traditional Tanzanian extended family system, having no children of one's own does not relieve one from the economic obligations to support the children of one's relatives and even friends. Children of relatives and friends pose equal demands as one's own children; and a person without children of his own faces even more numerous demands from children of relatives and friends.

Similarly, an individual who lacks personal means economically does not necessarily have his children economically doomed. All the relatives and friends who happen to be economically better off are required to come to his aid and save the children from their plight.

For this reason, the institution of priestly celibacy notwithstanding, the Catholic Church in Tanzania is actually facing a double problem: on the one hand, some priests who happen to fail in their vow of priestly celibacy manage to have the children thus begotten reared by their relatives without being economically overstrained themselves. This can easily encourage irresponsible parenthood in the true sense of the word.

On the other hand, economic demands from relatives and friends are pushing many a priest into all kinds of unacceptable economic involvements or into feeling inclined to misappropriate ecclesiastical funds for private family use. In this way, both the efforts of Emperor Justinian and the Gregorian reforms mentioned above become frustrated.

b. Priestly celibacy seen from the social point of view

From the social point of view, priestly celibacy seems to find even less backing from the surrounding human cultures. Both the Roman milieu and the accepted Jewish attitudes could not have inspired the early Church with the notion of priestly celibacy. On the contrary, relying on those surroundings would have proven a hindrance to any suggestion of the idea of priestly celibacy. To quote, once again, from the above mentioned article of J.M. Ford on celibacy:

> The practice of celibacy in the primitive Church was hindered for two reasons: (i) Jewish law required every healthy male to procreate; (ii) Roman law discouraged celibacy, placed penalties on bachelors and rewarded women who gave birth to three or more children.

It is a matter of fact that the urge to procreate is deeply engraved in human nature. It would, therefore, be a real surprise to find a human society which would engender practices discouraging the act of procreation. Periodical abstinence from sexual activity is a rather common practice in many ancient and present day societies. But the lifelong abstinence from marriage entailed in priestly celibacy has always been a socially rare commodity.

Even in the New Testament, in fact, there seems to be indications that presbyters (bishops) were expected to be married men. They needed to have proven themselves socially to be good leaders by managing their own families successfully in the eyes of their societies (cf e.g., 1 Tim 3:1-7).

In spite of the many modern efforts to discourage procreation on the pretext of the world's overpopulation, children continue to be highly valued in Tanzanian culture. Procreation remains a precious social value and will, seemingly, continue to be so for a long time still. Failure to procreate continues to be one of the greatest misfortunes in society that can befall an African man or woman. Because of social pressure, an unfruitful marital union will end up either in polygamy with all its concomitant unhappinesses or in marriage breakdown, an equally unfortunate event.

It would, therefore, be a frustrating attempt to try to justify or disapprove priestly celibacy in the cultural context of Africa from the social point of view. Priestly celibacy did not start off as a social prompting of any culture. This is a very important element to consider if we are not to become involved in other more complicated problems. When people speak so much of Christianity in Africa having paved the way for Western colonialism and the current propaganda for birth control as being Western malicious moves for new-colonialism, priestly celibacy must be shown not to be a cultural imposition.

The desire to fit priestly celibacy into social environments of given cultures is, at present, leading to strange solutions totally unacceptable as modes of inculturating the Catholic faith. Realizing that celibacy is unnatural to African culture, advocates of inculturation are proposing:

1. Total elimination of priestly celibacy in the Church of Africa. This is usually suggested to be done gradually such as by introducing and popularizing in a special way the married diaconate as a step towards married priests. Should we really sacrifice the values behind priestly celibacy for the sake of social demands of inculturation?

2. Introduction and acceptance of traditionally accepted marriages for priests; such marriages would, of course, have no significance for the Church but would be fully recognized in traditional society. There is no need to say that such practices would lead to double living for the priests involved. Before the Church they would be celibates, but before their traditional societies they would be married. There is no doubt that for such priests to remain truly celibate would be most difficult. But even if some were to remain faithful, what message would that syncretistic life bring to the community?

3. Introduction of spiritual marriages for the celibate Catholic priests. Such marriages should, preferably, be with women consecrated in virginity for the service of the Church so as to ensure spiritual inspirations on both sides. Of course, the concrete practicability of such marriages is very doubtful. But the main obstacle to such marriages from the doctrinal point of view is the dualism involved therein. The idea of a married spirit in a celibate body is a strange way of resolving the problem of priestly celibacy as a social problem for inculturation.

Priestly celibacy as a religious value

The real reason and basis for priestly celibacy in the Catholic Church has always been the religious one, and it must always remain so. Economic and social environments may be of some assistance to the realization of the religious reason as long as they are taken in subordinate relationship to the basic reason. Taken individually and in isolation from the religious basis, the social and economic reasons may even distort the true meaning of priestly celibacy reducing it to a meaningless, frustrating practice as we have been trying to show above. Yet, even the religious aspect of priestly celibacy must also be carefully and fundamentally analyzed and given proper orientation if it is to give the true meaning of that sacred institution.

In his Letter to the Corinthians (cf 1 Cor 7), St Paul had given instructions on the question of marriage or no marriage; instructions which, through misinterpretation, later led into quite questionable beliefs and practices. In 1 Corinthians 7:17, for example, St Paul writes: "Anyway let everyone continue in the part which the Lord has allotted to him as he was when God called him. This is the rule that I give to all the Churches." Basing themselves on this instruction of St Paul, some Syrian Church were to come up with, in the second and third centuries, with demands for baptism which required the decision on the part of any aspirant to baptism to opt for either marriage or celibacy before the conferring of the sacrament of baptism.

In their typical heretical way, the Manichaeans were later on to go even further to the extreme. For them only celibates were the real and full members of the Church. Those who were married or who intended to marry could not be received into full membership of the Church. They remained, as it were, perpetual catechumens.

Now, the sacrament of baptism is basic for human salvation (cf Mk 16:16). Through baptism the human person is graciously introduced into the history of salvation. By making celibacy a precondition for baptism, the Manichaeans came to make it the means of salvation within reach of human means.

In African culture, priestly celibacy considered from the religious point of view presents a theological problem just opposite to that of the Manicheans. Unlike the Manichaean dualist who wants to realize his own salvation by liberating the spirit from bodily imprisonment by abstaining from procreation, the African traditionalist in his religious faith believes that he can avoid having his life end up in a meaningless existence after his death by continuing to live in his children. The African traditional believer holds that a person who dies without begetting any children has no chance for a happy meaningful life beyond the grave. Thus failure to procreate is equivalent to failure to attain salvation in the life after death. Humanity is, through procreation, their own saviour. The saving role of Christ is thus rendered superfluous.

As the Holy Father, Pope John Paul II, put it, the true meaning of priestly celibacy is "profoundly connected with ordination whereby a man takes on the likeness of Jesus Christ", the true and only Saviour of humanity. By thus being connected with the person of Jesus Christ, priestly celibacy ceases to be a power for salvation independent of the only Saviour of mankind. It is no longer a merely negative act of self-denial; rather it is an act of self-giving to and in union with Christ.

In the same way, as that act of taking on the likeness of Jesus Christ, priestly celibacy for the African ceases to lead to self-destruction, to a meaningless existence devoid of real life. Rather, it leads to the person of Jesus Christ who is "the Way, the Truth and the Life" (cf Jn 14:6).

Conclusion

Priestly celibacy will continue to pose problems with regard to any efforts of inculturation. However, many of these problems are due either to a lack of appreciation for the profound religious meaning of celibacy or due to a misunderstanding of the true meaning of inculturation. When human cultural values take the upper hand, theology and faith become distorted. Instead of human culture being converted to the Christian faith, it attempts to convert the faith itself. In this question of priestly celibacy, it is imperative for everyone concerned to be aware of the profound religious meaning of the institution.

The Oriental Rite Churches and priestly celibacy

Julianus Voronovsky

Titular Archbishop of Deulto
Auxiliary of Lvov of the Ukrainians

To avoid drawing facile conclusions when speaking of the esteem which priestly celibacy enjoys in the Catholic East, we must not forget what a large number of different, individual Churches there are, each with its own history and tradition. Each of these many Churches has its own approach to this complex subject and stresses differing aspects of it. And this makes it difficult to treat them all at once, unlike the history of the Western Church.

This notwithstanding, we can certainly speak of characteristics common to all the Oriental Churches, in that their canonical discipline springs from a common legislative source, back in the early centuries of Christian history. Furthermore, there have been mutual influences and direct derivations; for all the present-day 21 Oriental Catholic Churches are derived from the five great traditions or so-called primary rites: the Alexandrian, the Antiochene, the Byzantine, the Chaldaean and the Armenian.[1]

In spite of this large number of individual or *sui iuris* Churches (to use the canonical term), certain things are common to all of them. We can say, while bearing in mind that these can only be general statements, each Church having its own practical and specific way of showing its esteem for priestly celibacy, which is generally speaking favoured in their ecclesial life.

According to historical sources, until the fourth century, ecclesiastical discipline was the same in the Eastern and Western Church, and the celibacy of the clergy was honoured without there being any particular canon law about it. Clerical celibacy and clerical marriage, even for bishops, were matters of personal choice. The primitive Church did not insist on the choice of celibacy, which was lived within the community as a grace or charism.

Preference for virginity, or renunciation of marriage in perfect and perpetual sexual continence for the sake of the kingdom of heaven, undoubtedly owed its origin to Jesus Christ's own teaching, clearly set down by St Matthew, the evangelist.[2] This preference was lived by Jesus himself, setting an example to be followed. In the East, there are no deeper or more fully significant reasons, theologically speaking, for justifying celibacy in all its aspects than the teaching delivered and lived by Jesus Christ.

The apostles were the first to accept the message and imitate the Master. The first one of all, so tradition avers, was St John the Apostle, followed by the Apostle Paul.[3] The latter, in his First Letter to the Corinthians, gives a pregnant piece of advice, applied in masterly manner on the practical plane: the appropriateness of giving oneself with undivided heart to the service of the Lord for one's neighbour. "The unmarried man is anxious about the affairs of the Lord, how to please the Lord; but the married man is anxious about worldly affairs, how to please his wife, and his interests are divided."[4]

This superior state of virginity consecrated to Christ came to be regarded throughout the Church as that most suitable for reaching Christian perfection. Such was to be the consistent teaching in the writings of the Fathers of the Church, both Eastern and Western. Despite the fact that in the first phase of Church history the direct connection between virginity and priesthood, as it came to be conceived of later, had not been clearly defined, a considerable number of Church Fathers forcefully recommended either abstinence from the use of marriage, or virginity, to the clergy, thus establishing the close connection existing between vocation to the ministerial priesthood and celibacy.[5]

From the fourth century onwards, the problem arises

113

over continence in the married state for married clergy with regard to celebrating the Divine Liturgy. Such difficulties, whether practical or doctrinal, were to be a matter for dispute and disagreement, manifested in the early ecumenical councils and various regional synods held by the Church, and also in various regions and ecclesiastical provinces. It should be noted that, according to the testimony of the Greek historian Socrates, no general law on continence existed even towards the middle of the fifth century when, only in certain areas, such as Macedonia, Thessaly and Hellas, it started to be introduced.

The question of continence is undoubtedly conditioned by influences stemming from Old Testament norms with regard to the continence required for those who devote themselves to liturgical prayer,[6] as also by cultural conditions of the period. Suffice it, for instance, to consider Pythagorism, Stoicism and certain kinds of Gnosticism which held body, sex and emotions in contempt. But mainly it has its origins in the deep theological, spiritual and ascetic reflection of the Fathers and the spiritual masters.

Discussion of this problem at synods and the decisions taken there had the effect that the discipline of priestly celibacy tended to assume fixed forms in ecclesiastical legislation. At the same time, however, it marked a divergence in discipline between East and West.

The route taken by the West as regards virginity or priestly celibacy, having traversed various partial stages of legislation with frequent inconsistencies between the law laid down and the practice observed, begins with the permanent exclusion of conjugal relations for ministers of religion. That is to say, with the obligation of continence on clerics from the moment of major ordination, on pain of deposition.[7] To end eventually with the clear discipline of celibacy, that is to say, with the exclusion from major orders of men bound by the marriage tie.[8]

However, the route taken by the East has been governed firmly by two principles: prohibition of marriage after ordination on pain of deposition, and retention of conjugal rights over the wife, whom it is not lawful to repudiate, for those men who are married before being ordained.[9]

Significantly therefore, there is no doctrinal difference between the Eastern and Western Church in regarding virginity and celibacy as the choice of a more perfect life. As regards the celibacy of priests, differing legislation has come into being, establishing in the one Church celibacy as obligatory by law on all those to receive Holy Orders, and in the other the option of being celibate or married.

Here questions arise over this difference. Is it due to a different way of grasping or interpreting the Sacred Scriptures? Is it due to a different apostolic tradition? Do virginity or priestly celibacy not enjoy the same esteem in either Church? The answers we shall give in explanation of this difference will show the depth of real esteem which priestly celibacy enjoys in the Oriental Churches.

First, we should point out that, during the first four centuries of Christian history constituting the common source for the whole Church, there existed in embryonic form, so to speak, all the elements fully justifying later legislation, as much for the East as for the West. These were the seeds of subsequent development, which took differing forms owing to stress and importance laid on differing elements. So, one may say that, if the law of celibacy, as such, is late, its meaning is certainly not so, nor justification of the obligation, nor the option of being a married priest in the East.

In fact, the difference lies only in the practical sphere, the product of two contrasting ecclesiastical worlds, with different mentalities and different ways of seeing things. The contrast was already to be seen in the first two synods to mark the branching of the routes taken by the East and West, that is to say, the Provincial Synod of Elvira and the Council of Nicaea.

At the Council of Nicaea in AD 325, the first ecumenical council of the Church, the Latin delegates presented a proposal to introduce the obligation of continence for the clergy throughout the Church. Undoubtedly, the Synod

Fathers esteemed and respected continence and virginity in accordance with shared, apostolic doctrine. The presence in the various diocese of priests observing continence, i.e. celibates, did not give any grounds for uneasiness. On the contrary, as St Paul had written, they were in fact able to devote themselves more to the Lord's affairs. But even so, the proposal was not approved, and in this the Council of Nicaea did not follow the dispositions of the Provincial Synod of Elvira, which had taken place in AD 306 and had, in its own region, decreed: "*Placuit in totum prohibere episcopis, presbyteris et diaconibus vel omnibus clericis positis in ministerio abstinere se a coniugibus suis et generare filios: quicumque vero ferit ab honore clericatus exterminentur.*"[10]

The reason for this rejection lay mainly in the different mentality of Latins and Greeks, a difference eloquently manifest in the unfolding of the two synods in question. At Elvira, only Latins were present, whereas at Nicaea the majority consisted of Eastern bishops, especially Greek ones.[11] Thus, at the first synod, the Latin conception was able fully to appear, and at the second, the Greek conception prevailed. Both unquestionably sought the best solution for the problems afflicting the Church of the day.

Behind these differing views of the problems and their possible solutions, one cannot but detect the influence of the social environment and the socio-economic problems to which the two Churches were subjected. For these would be a further factor in determining the varying attitudes adopted.

To put the matter in a nutshell, as regards the celibacy of priests we may say that one conception mainly stresses that aspect according to which it is better to marry than to burn;[12] and the other, the judgement that "he who marries does well, and he who does not marry does *better*".[13] The consequences stem from this.

Here it is important to emphasize that the East is very conservative and traditional, and this decision taken at the Council of Nicaea, codifying previous common practice, set a deep stamp on all subsequent legislation, which was faithfully to be maintained until the Trullan Council (692), which constituted the last word, still in force up till now, in the matter of ecclesiastical celibacy in the East, only confirmed the practice deriving from the decision of the first ecumenical council of Nicaea.

The Trullan Council was, in a certain sense, a step forward if one considers that it established the obligation of absolute continence for the bishop, and the duty of definitely parting company with his wife if he had one and of assigning her to some convent far away from the episcopal residence, or, if she wished and was considered worthy, of promoting her to be a deaconess.[14] This clearly demonstrates and confirms the esteem enjoyed by priestly celibacy in the East, for it obliges to celibacy the bishops, i.e., those who properly speaking possess the apex and fullness of the priesthood.

Marriage for the secular clergy, and promotion to the episcopate reserved to monks, who by choice of monastic life are celibate, is a practice that only entered the Eastern Churches after the grievous break with ecclesial unity which occurred in 1054. It will be for the Churches of the East to find their way back to unity with the Bishop of Rome, while respecting the ancient practice of the Church established at the Trullan Council, that is to say, freedom of choice for candidates to the priesthood, for the secular clergy. For this possibility has been made available by the Catholic Church's intention to maintain the traditions of each individual Church intact.

From these various points, we can state that celibacy enjoys the same esteem in the East as it does in the West and, because it is so appreciated, the principle is maintained unchanged of the voluntary aspect, constituting the fundamental element in the mentality and spirituality of the East. This factor, however, means that training for celibacy takes a prime role in the arduous task of preparing candidates properly for Holy Orders, depending of course on which specific road they propose to take.

In conclusion, canonical legislation apart, it is encouraging to see what a large number of priests embrace celibacy in the normal life of these Churches. Wherever you go, you will see that the people of God show the highest esteem for priests who consecrate themselves completely, in total generosity, to the service of the Church.

NOTES

1. Cf *Enchiridion Vaticanum* 12, Bologna 1990, 892-893.
2. Mt 19:12.
3. 1 Cor 7:7.
4. 1 Cor 7:32-33.
5. Cf Tertullian, *De exhort. castitatis*, c.13; PL 2, 930, 993; St Epiphanius, *Adv. haer.*, II, 48, 9 & 59, 4; PG 41, 869, 1025; Eusebius of Caesarea, *Demonstr. evan.*, I, 9; PC 22, 81; St Cyril of Jerusalem, *Catechesis* 12, 25; PG 33, 757; St Gregory of Nyssa, *De Virginitate*, PC 13, 318-382; St John Chrysostom, *De Sacerdotio*, 1. III, 4; PG 48, 642.
6. 1 Cor 7:5.
7. Cf Synod of Elvira (305) c. 33; Synod of Rome (386).
8. Cf Lateran I (1123) cc. 7, 21; Lateran II (1139) c. 7.
9. *Canones Apostolorum* (4th cent.) cc. 6, 26; Ancyra c. 10; Gangra (340) c. 4; Trullus (692) cc. 6, 13.
10. Mansi 11, II.
11. De C. Clercq, *Fontes Iuridici Ecclesiarum Orientalium*, Rome 1967, 20-21.
12. 1 Cor 7:8.
13. Cf 1 Cor 7:38.
14. Trullus (692) cc. 12, 48.

The Orthodox Churches and priestly celibacy

Damaskinos Papandreou

Orthodox Metropolitan of Switzerland

> "Priesthood... according to the
> canonical tradition in force,
> constitutes an impediment to marriage."

The Orthodox position on marriage and clerical celibacy has been fixed by the long patristic tradition and practice of the Church as regards the profound theological content of the sacrament of marriage and the eminently personal spirituality of the discipline of celibacy. Marriage according to the Lord and celibacy for the Lord's sake are two different spiritual paths, it is true, but both are incontestably valid for a true living of the content of the faith.

Of these paths, anyone is free to follow either the one or the other in accordance with his own vocation and particular charisms. The Church equally blesses the two manifestations of the Christian's spiritual combat, and Orthodox Churches show no preference for one at the expense of the other, preferring not to advance theological reasons in justification of one option rather than another. The choice lies with individual Christians, who thus make themselves responsible for the consequences of their own spiritual combat.

This awareness on the Church's part was fixed in patristic tradition from earliest times, with special reference to the personal freedom of the faithful in choosing what spiritual combat they would undertake. According to Clement of Alexandria, "celibacy and marriage each have their own functions and specific services to the Lord."[1] Because of this, "we pay homage to those whom the Lord has favoured with the gift of celibacy and admire monogamy and its dignity."[2]

In the same spirit and context, Clement censured the Gnostics who considered marriage to be a sin: "If lawful marriage is a sin, I do not see how anyone can claim to know God while saying the Lord's commandment is a sin; indeed, the law being sacred, marriage is too. Hence the Apostle relates this sacrament to Christ and the Church."[3]

Putting the personal charism of celibacy into practice, the apostolic and patristic tradition regard as a personal gift from God. Those, therefore, who have chosen the celibate life have no right to pride themselves over the superiority of their spiritual combat: "If anyone can persevere in chastity in honour of the Lord's flesh, let him do so without boasting about it. If he prides himself in this, he is lost; and if he tells anyone else about it except his own bishop, he is corrupt."[4] This personal charism is freely received and this spiritual combat is freely chosen. It cannot be imposed. It is not demanded by the nature of priesthood. The Church may require it for certain ministries. The Western Church requires it for those who are called to be priests and bishops. The Orthodox Church requires it, for pastoral reasons, for those who are called to be bishops.

Thus Orthodox tradition and practice honour and respect the celibacy of priests and praise their service in the body of the Church; at the same time, they honour and respect the married clergy since, they too, serve the same sacrament of the Church and salvation. The Orthodox Church thus accepts these two forms of service equally and leaves the choice of which it is to be to the individual member, in accordance with his own vocation and particular charisms. For pastoral reasons however, the Church has favoured the institution of celibacy for the order of bishops, and these are chosen exclusively from the celibate priesthood.

Until the schism between the two Churches, the Latin discipline concerning obligatory clerical celibacy was not regarded as a serious theological or ecclesiastical divergence, since neither of the two forms of service seemed to run counter to the tradition of the Church. This positive attitude on the part of the Eastern Church is clearly seen in canon 3 of the Council *in Trullo*, which underscores the need to make "pure and blameless ministers, worthy of the spiritual sacrifice of the Great God at once Victim and Priest, out of all those inscribed in the ranks of the clergy and through whom the graces of the sacraments pass to men, and the need to purge them of the filthiness of their illicit marriages; since, however, those of the most holy Roman Church propose to follow the discipline very strictly, while those of this imperial and God-protected city prefer the rule of humanity and indulgence, we have fused the two tendencies into one, lest mildness degenerate into licentiousness or austerity into bitterness..."

The combination of these two free spiritual choices constitutes the absolute theological criterion of the Orthodox tradition which, though susceptible to differing pastoral adaptations in local Churches between 'severity' and 'indulgence', cannot be invalidated by these adaptations. On the other hand, the theological principle that no sacrament of the Church can exclude the believer from participating in another sacrament of the Church is constant and incontestable, except where a personal spiritual choice on the part of the individual is concerned, or a particular charism is given the individual by God. Nonetheless, the theological or moral censure of the one or other form of ecclesiastical service, as has occurred since the Great Schism (1054), gives a theological content to legitimate differences of pastoral practice between 'mildness' and 'austerity'.

It should be noted that the second pre-conciliar, pan-Orthodox conference, which met in Chambésy at the Orthodox Centre of the Ecumenical Patriarchate from 3 September to 12 September 1982, took the following decisions on the topic of impediments to marriage (decisions having no canonical force until the Great and Holy Synod has pronounced on them): "With regard to monks, who by virtue of the religious tonsure may not marry, the possibility is suggested that they may enter into marriage if, having resigned their religious identity whether willingly or unwillingly in the case of *force majeure*, they have been reduced to the lay state."

"Priesthood, in all three of its degrees, according to the canonical tradition in force (canon 3 of the Council *in Trullo*), constitutes an impediment to marriage."

NOTES

1. *Strom.*, III, 12.
2. *Ibid.*, III, 4.
3. *Ibid.*, III, 12.
4. *Letter of Ignatius to Polycarp*, V, 1, 2.

The Anglican Communion and priestly celibacy

David Michael Hope

Bishop of London

The requirement for celibacy in the clergy was formally abolished in the Church of England in 1549. Since that time, and continuing in the present time, there is no requirement for celibacy even among single clergy within the Anglican Communion. Indeed, the point has been made again only very recently in the report from the House of Bishops, on Human Sexuality, that "celibacy cannot be prescribed for anyone. What is needed is that the single should live in the form of chastity appropriate to their situation."

In one sense, I suppose I conclude my presentation here and now. But that would be to do an injustice to all those clergy who have lived and continue to live the celibate life, among whom I would count myself to be one. For us in the Church of England, and indeed in the Anglican Communion as a whole, there is the frustration that nowhere is there the availability of any publicly recognized form of commitment to such a state. Some individual clergy are associated in some way or another, either as members of a third order or oblates or associates with a religious community, and that association may contain a commitment to celibacy as part of the rule which is agreed between the community and the individual. Some seek to make a more formal commitment on a regular basis before a bishop, seeking possibilities of renewal on a three-year or five-year basis; others make a commitment for life. But it has to be said all such arrangements are to that extent informal. There continues to be no recognition of the celibate state of the clergy.

Undoubtedly, the rise of the religious orders in the wake of the Oxford Movement in the Church of England in the last century insured the re-establishing of lives in community dedicated to the evangelical counsels of poverty, chastity and obedience. The current Directory of the religious life for the Church of England speaks of poverty, chastity and obedience as being primarily ascetical spiritual aspirations. It goes on to spell out what it means when it speaks of the vow of chastity – "the religious seeks freedom to devote the self entirely and directly to Christ in singleness of heart. Celibacy is the distinguishing external characteristic of the vow of chastity. By seeking to serve God in celibacy, the religious witnesses to the imminence of the kingdom of God and to its absolute claims on all human life". A number of the earliest 'sisterhoods' and 'brotherhoods' were certainly misunderstood, and a source of diversion and amusement for some time. Nevertheless, soon they became established, and a considerable force for spiritual renewal within the Church of England and again more widely throughout the Anglican Communion. It is through an association with religious communities that many, both men and women, particularly those who are single, have found a strong bond and fellowship by way of support for their celibate state.

However, to make the point that there is no formal recognition of the celibate state does not imply there are no clear standards or expectations for the ordering of the lives of clergy, be they married or single. The Ordinal itself either of the 1662 Prayer Book or the Alternative Service Book of the Church of England make very clear the demands upon behaviour, public and private, which the Church expects of its ordained ministers.

The 'charge' from the ordaining Bishop to those to be ordained deacon or priest, as well as the questions put by him to all the candidates, speaks clearly of the wholesome pattern and example which they must be to those among whom they exercise their ministry. The Book of Common Prayer speaks both of the 'excellency' and of the 'difficulty' of the priestly office, recognizing that the expectations of the Church are well nigh impossible, and indeed that it will be quite impossible in and of one's own strength and powers ever to live up to this ideal – "therefore ye ought, and have need, to pray earnestly for the Holy Spirit." To this end all worldly cares and studies are to be put aside so that the individual's life may be rooted and grounded in prayer and the study of the Holy Scriptures; the word of God thus forming and fashioning the "manners both of yourselves and of them that specially pertain unto you".

This theme is taken up again in the direct questioning of the bishop to the ordinances, both in the Book of Common Prayer and in the Alternative Service Book where they are asked directly: "Will you strive to fashion your own life and that of your household according to the way of Christ?". The same theme is underlined in a paragraph of the bishop's charge in the Alternative Service Book "because you cannot bear the weight of this ministry in your own strength but only by the grace and power of God, pray earnestly for his Holy Spirit. Pray that he will each day enlarge and enlighten your understanding of the Scriptures, so that you may grow stronger and more mature in your ministry, as you fashion your life, and the lives of your people, on the word of God." The candidates are further encouraged to give themselves 'wholly' to God's service, to "devote to him your best powers of mind and spirit so that as you daily follow the rule and teaching of Our Lord, with the heavenly assistance of his Holy Spirit, you may grow up into his likeness, and sanctify the lives of all with whom you have to do."

Although, however, there is nothing here said explicitly about celibacy, there is nevertheless a clear standard for all those ordained, either married or single, that they are to use positively and creatively all that God has given them, including the gift of sex, for the purposes which he has intended, and that their giving of themselves 'wholly' in their ministerial office and work will be a sign that they are so committed. And that all the time their ministerial lives are to be rooted and grounded in a spirituality which is nurtured in Word and Sacrament.

This grounding in a spirituality of Word and Sacrament is reflected in the canonical provision for clergy, more particularly in Canon C26 – *Of the manner of life of ministers* – where it is clearly stated that every bishop, priest and deacon "is under obligation" not being let by sickness or some other urgent cause to say daily the morning and evening prayer, either privately or openly: and to celebrate the Holy Communion, or be present thereat, on all Sundays and other principal feast days. He is also to be diligent in daily prayer and intercession, in examination of his conscience, and in the study of the Holy Scriptures and such other studies as pertain to his ministerial duties. Arising from this firm basis, there are echoes in the Canon of expectations of the ordinal with regard to the person's manner of life. For the Canon stipulates that "a minister shall not give himself to such occupations, habits, or recreations as do not befit his sacred calling, or may be detrimental to the performance of the duties of his office, or tend to be a just cause for offence to others; and at all times he shall be diligent to frame and fashion his life and that of his family according to the doctrine of Christ, and to make himself and them, as much as in him lies, wholesome examples and patterns to the flock of Christ".

Whether then the ordained minister is married or single, it is clear from this brief review of the norms which the Ordinal and the Canons set out that the ordering of a person's life including the sexual, is part of that process begun in baptism whereby we are enabled both to die with Christ, but also to rise with him into a new way of life. And it is this altogether more positive view of sex and sexuality which I believe needs to be commended as the possibility of celibacy is set before those to be ordained. Generally speaking it has had a bad press because it has been and continues to be often understood in terms of negativity and denial. And yet as the House of Bishops report on Human

Sexuality sets out: "It is increasingly recognized in the Churches today that celibacy is a special gift and calling of the Holy Spirit in accordance with Jesus' own words in Matthew 19:12 ... celibacy is thus a choice of the unmarried state not for self-regarding reasons but from love in order to be able to serve God and neighbour more freely, whether through the life of prayer or through activity or both." The House of Bishop's statement however is equally clear that celibacy ought not either to be assumed or imposed upon the single person. It ought to be a deliberate choice and act of the individual.

One of the major issues at the present time centres around the ordination of the homosexual person. This was one of the main themes of the House of Bishops report on Human Sexuality. The bishops concluded that the very fact that a person is homosexual by orientation should be no bar to ordination. Indeed, the bishops recognized that "we know for a fact that the ministries of many homophile clergy are highly dedicated and have been greatly blessed. God has endowed them with spiritual gifts, as he has his other ministers, and we give thanks for all alike." Further when such a person wishes it to be known more publicly that they are homophile in orientation, but who are nevertheless committed to a life of abstinence – a life lived in the power of the Holy Spirit and out of love for Christ, a life of great faithfulness, travelled often under the weight of a very heavy cross – such a person ought to be accepted and supported by the Church in every way possible. However, the bishops concluded that because of the distinctive nature of their calling, status and consecration, there were inevitably certain restrictions upon clergy which were not necessarily incumbent upon laity, and one such restriction was the possibility of living in a sexually active homophile relationship. Needless to say, there is much discussion over this last mentioned matter and there continues to be widely divergent and differing points of view held and expressed within the Church of England at the present time.

Given that celibacy is not enjoined on any ordained

127

person in the Church of England, there is nevertheless no doubt about the Church's expectation with regard to chastity both for married and unmarried clergy, and for the single person whatever their sexual orientation may be. Moreover, this is not seen to be a negative disavowal of the gift of sex, but rather a positive movement of the whole person, sexuality and all, into the maturity and fullness of life which Christ wills for all people, and upon which, in baptism, we are already entered. The Church exists to live out in the world the truth it has been given about the nature of God's creation, the way of redemption through the cross and the ultimate hope of resurrection and fullness of life. All clergy, as consecrated public and representative figures, themselves entrusted with the message and the means of grace, have a responsibility on behalf of the whole body of Christ to show the primacy of this truth by striving to embody it in their own lives. The way often may be problematic and difficult, a way of frustration and struggle, truly the way of the cross. But then those who follow faithfully in the way of the cross find in it not only their Lord's resurrection but their own also – the way of the resurrection, the way of joy and of life eternal.

Purity and the priesthood in the Hebrew Scriptures and Rabbinic tradition

Jacob Neusner

Distinguished Research Professor of Religious Studies
University of South Florida

The Book of Leviticus makes explicit the requirements that priests who ministered at the holy ark in the Tent of Meeting, that is, in the Temple of Jerusalem, had to attain the status of purity. That requirement affected every dimension of their lives, from birth through marriage to death. They had to exhibit proper genealogical credentials. They had to marry women who met a certain standard. When they entered the Temple, they had to have purified themselves in accord with the Levitical regulations. When they actually conducted the rites of sacrifice and offered up the consecrated portions, they had to meet these same standards. And, of course, when they consumed their share of the holy offerings, they and their families had to meet these same high standards.

The sources of uncleanness are specified in Leviticus 11-15 and Numbers 19. These include unclean animals, improperly slaughtered animals, certain bodily excretions, sexual activity (seminal emissions), and the like, as well as the corpses. Rites of purification, furthermore, are fully spelled out in context, washing with water (in an immersion pool), use of purification-water (Numbers 19), and so on. Priests could serve only if they were bodily whole and complete; they could contract corpse uncleanness only for immediate family members; they had to keep the foods set aside for their consumption pure and had to eat those foods with purified utensils. In these and numerous other ways, the written Torah spells out the conviction that the priesthood is required to preserve purity in the Temple rites and in personal life as well. There is no priesthood that can function unless the purity laws are observed.

Rabbinic literature, represented by the Mishnah, ca. AD 200, a philosophical law code that stands at the head of all the documents of the oral Torah, takes for granted that the purity laws of Leviticus and Numbers apply to all Israelites, not only to the members of the priestly caste. A brief account of the way in which the Rabbinic law treats the topic suffices.

The connection between the priesthood and purity stands behind the entire Rabbinic treatment of those two subjects: there is no priesthood without purity, and there is no service of God without the Temple and the offerings presented by that priesthood. The reason is simple. The oral Torah, represented by the Mishnah, sets forth a theory of the life of Israel that centres on the sanctification of God's people, and that is meant in a concrete and worldly way. Sanctification being the goal, purity is a principal means toward that end. This is stated in so many words in an account of the place of purity and of sanctification on the scale of the Torah's requirements:

> R. Pinhas b. Yair says, "Heedfulness leads to (hygienic) cleanliness, cleanliness leads to cultic cleanness, cultic cleanness leads to abstinence, abstinence leads to holiness, holiness leads to modesty, modesty leads to the fear of sin, the fear of sin leads to piety, piety leads to the Holy Spirit, the Holy Spirit leads to the resurrection of the dead, and the resurrection of the dead comes through Elijah, blessed be his memory. Amen." (Mishnah-Tractate Sotah 9:15).

What we see, therefore, is that there is an integral connection between purity – which invariably means the purity of the cult, the Temple, and the priesthood of Israel – and sanctification.

The tractates of the Mishnah concerning purity are these: Kelim (susceptibility of utensils to uncleanness); Ohalot (transmission of corpse-uncleanness in the tent of a corpse); Negaim (the uncleanness described in Leviticus 13-14); Parah (the preparation of purification-water); Tohorot (problems of doubt in connection with matters of cleanness); Miqvaot (immersion-pools); Niddah (menstrual uncleanness); Makhshirin (rendering susceptible to uncleanness produce that is dry and so not susceptible); Zabim (the uncleanness mentioned in Leviticus 15); Tebul-Yom (the uncleanness of one who has immersed on that self-same day and awaits sunset for completion of the purification rites); Yadayim (the uncleanness of hands); Uqsin (the uncleanness transmitted through what is connected to unclean produce).

In volume, the sixth division, devoted to Purities, covers approximately a quarter of the entire Mishnah. Topics of interest to the priesthood and the Temple, such as priestly fees, conduct of the cult on holy days, conduct of the cult on ordinary days and management and upkeep of the Temple, and the rules of cultic cleanness, predominate in the first, second, fifth and sixth divisions, in volume well over two-thirds of the whole. Rules governing the social order form the bulk of the third and fourth.

The stress of the Mishnah throughout on the priestly caste and the Temple cult point to the document's principal concern, which centred upon sanctification, understood as the correct arrangement of all things, each in its proper category, each called by its rightful name, just as at the creation as portrayed in the Priestly document, and just as with the cult itself as set forth in Leviticus. Further, the thousands of rules and cases (with sages' disputes thereon) that comprise the document, upon close reading, turn out to express in concrete language abstract principles of hierarchical classification.

These define the document's method and mark it as a work of a philosophical character. Not only so, but a variety of specific, recurrent concerns, for example, the relationship of being to becoming, actual to potential, the principles of economics, politics, correspond point by point to comparable ones in Graeco-Roman philosophy, particularly Aristotle's tradition. This stress on proper order and right rule and the formulation of a philosophy, politics and economics, within the principles of natural history set forth by Aristotle, explain why the Mishnah makes a statement to be classified as philosophy, concerning the order of the natural world in its correspondence with the supernatural world.

The system of philosophy expressed through concrete and detailed law presented by the Mishnah, consists of a coherent logic and topic, a cogent world-view and comprehensive way of living. It is a world-view which speaks of transcendent things, a way of life in response to the sanctification of Israel in deed and in deliberation. Sanctification thus means two things: first, distinguishing Israel in all its dimensions from the world in all its ways; second, establishing the stability, order, regularity, predictability and reliability of Israel in the world of nature and supernature, in particular at moments and in contexts of danger. Danger means instability, disorder, irregularity, uncertainty and betrayal. Each topic of the system as a whole takes up a critical and indispensable moment or context of social being. Through what is said in regard to each of the Mishnah's principal topics, what the system expressed through normative rules as a whole wishes to declare is fully expressed. Yet if the parts severally and jointly give the message of the whole, the whole cannot exist without all of the parts, so well joined and carefully crafted are they all. These general remarks bring us back to the topic at hand: purity, the priesthood, the Temple, and the cult.

The Division of Purities presents a very simple system of three principal parts: sources of uncleanness, objects and substances susceptible to uncleanness, and modes of purification from uncleanness. So it tells the story of what makes a given sort of object unclean and what makes it clean. Viewed as a whole, the Division of Purities treats the interplay of persons, food and liquids. Dry inanimate objects or food are not susceptible to uncleanness. What is wet is susceptible. So liquids activate the system. What is unclean, moreover, emerges from uncleanness through the operation of liquids specifically, through immersion in fit water of requisite volume and in natural condition. Liquids thus deactivate the system. Thus, water in its natural condition is what concludes the process by removing uncleanness. Water in its unnatural condition, that is, deliberately affected by human agency, is what imparts susceptibility to uncleanness to begin with. The uncleanness of persons, furthermore, is signified by body liquids or flux in the case of the menstruating woman and the *zab* (the person suffering from the form of uncleanness described in Leviticus 15:1ff). Corpse uncleanness is conceived to be a kind of effluent, a viscous gas, which flows like liquid. Utensils for their part receive uncleanness when they form receptacles able to contain liquid.

In sum, we have a system in which the invisible flow of fluid-like substances or powers serve to put food, drink and receptacles into the status of uncleanness and to remove those things from that status. Whether or not we call the system 'metaphysical', it certainly has no material base but is conditioned upon highly abstract notions. Thus in material terms, the effect of liquid is upon food, drink, utensils, and people. The consequence has to do with who may eat and drink what food and liquid, and what food and drink may be consumed in which pots and pans. These loci are specified by tractates on utensils and on food and drink.

The human being is ambivalent. Persons fall in the middle, between sources and loci of uncleanness, because they are both. They serve as sources of uncleanness. They also become unclean. The *zab*, suffering the uncleanness described in Leviticus chapter 15, the menstruating woman, the woman after childbirth, and the person afflicted with the skin ailment described in Leviticus chapters 13 and 14 – all are sources of uncleanness. But being unclean, they fall within the system's loci, its programme of consequences.

So they make other things unclean and are subject to penalties because they are unclean. Unambiguous sources of uncleanness never also constitute *loci* affected by uncleanness. They always are unclean and never can become clean: the corpse, the dead creeping thing, and things like them. Inanimate sources of uncleanness and inanimate objects are affected by uncleanness. Systematically unique, people and liquids have the capacity to inaugurate the process of uncleanness (as sources) and also are subject to those same processes (as objects of uncleanness).

Where the Mishnah moves beyond Scripture – the oral Torah beyond the written – is in its premise that the purity laws concern not only the cult and the Temple, but also the home and the heart. The ideas ultimately expressed in the Mishnah began among people who had a special interest in observing cultic cleanness, as dictated by the Priestly Code. There can be no doubt, moreover, that the context for such cleanness is the home, not solely the Temple, about which Leviticus speaks. The issues of the law leave no doubt on that score. Since priests ate heave offerings at home, and did so in a state of cultic cleanness, it was a small step to apply the same taboos to food which was not a consecrated gift to the priests.

What is said through the keeping of these laws is that the food eaten at home, not deriving from the altar and its provision for the priesthood of meat not burned up in the fire, was as holy as the meal offerings, meat offerings, and drink offerings, consecrated by being set aside for the altar and then, in due course, partly given to the priests and partly tossed on the altar and burned up. If food not consecrated for the altar, not protected in a state of cleanness (in the case of wheat), or carefully inspected for blemishes (in the case of beasts), and not eaten by priests in the Temple, was deemed subject to the same purity-restrictions as food consecrated for the altar, this carries implications about the character of that food, those who were to eat it, and the conditions in which it was grown and eaten. First, all food, not only that for the altar, was to be protected in a state of

Levitical cleanness, thus holiness, that is, separateness. Second, the place in the Land, in which the food was grown and kept was to be kept cultically clean, holy, just like the Temple. Third, the people, Israel, who were to eat that food were holy, just like the priesthood, in rank behind the Temple's chief caste. Fourth, the act of eating food anywhere in the Holy Land was analogous to the act of eating food in the Temple, by the altar.

The purity of the priesthood therefore symbolized the sanctification of all Israel – that is the proposition implicit in the laws of the Mishnah. All of these obvious inferences point to a profound conviction about the Land, people, produce, condition, and context of nourishment. The setting was holy. The actors were holy. And what, specifically, they did which had to be protected in holiness was eating. For when they ate their food at home, they ate it the way priests did in the Temple. And the way priests ate their food in the Temple, that is, the cultic rules and conditions observed in that setting, was like the way God ate his food in the Temple. That is to say, God's food and locus of nourishment were to be protected from the same sources of danger and contamination, preserved in the same exalted condition and sanctification. So by acting, that is, eating like God, Israel became like God: a pure and perfect incarnation, on earth in the Land which was holy, of the model of heaven. Eating food was the critical act and occasion, just as the priestly authors of Leviticus and Numbers had maintained when they made laws governing slaughtering beasts and burning up their flesh, baking pancakes and cookies with and without olive oil and burning them on the altar, pressing grapes and making wine and pouring it out onto the altar. The nourishment of the Land – meat, grain, oil, and wine – was set before God and burned ('offered up') in conditions of perfect cultic antisepsis.

In context, this antisepsis provided protection against things deemed the opposite of nourishment, the quintessence of death: corpse matter, people who looked like corpses (Leviticus 13), dead creeping things, blood when not flowing in the veins of the living, such as menstrual blood (Leviticus 15), other sorts of flux (semen in men, non-menstrual blood in women) which yield not life but then its opposite, so death. What these excrescences have in common, of course, is that they are ambivalent. Why? Because they may be one thing or the other. Blood in the living is the soul; blood not in the living is the soul of contamination. The corpse was once a living person, like God; the person with skin like a corpse's and who looks dead was once a person who looked alive; the flux of the *zab* (Leviticus 15) comes from the flaccid penis which under the right circumstances, that is properly erect, produces semen and makes life. What is at the margin between life and death and can go either way is what is the source of uncleanness. But that is insufficient. For the opposite, in the Priestly Code, of unclean is not only clean, but also holy. The antonym is not to be missed: death or life, unclean or holy.

So the cult is the point of struggle between the forces of life and nourishment and the forces of death and extinction: meat, grain, oil and wine, against corpse matter, dead creeping things, blood in the wrong setting, semen in the wrong context, and the like. Then, on the occasions when meat was eaten, mainly, at the time of festivals or other moments at which sin offerings and peace offerings were made, people who wished to live ate their meat, and at all times ate the staples of wine, oil, and bread, in a state of life and so generated life. They kept their food and themselves away from the state of death as much as possible. And this heightened reality pertained at home as much as in the Temple, where most people rarely went on ordinary days. The Temple was the font of life, the bulwark against death, and the purity of the priesthood formed the Temple's guarantee of sanctification.

An Oriental Church returns to unity choosing priestly celibacy

Benedict Varghese Gregorios Thangalathil

Archbishop of Trivandrum (Syro-Malankara)

Origins of the Church of India

It was a singular act of divine providence that the Good News of salvation was preached in India by the Apostle, St Thomas, not long after the resurrection of the Lord. In this country, situated far away from the great centres of Christianity, the growth of the faith was very slow. However, the Christian community remained united until the sixteenth century. Due to certain vicissitudes of history, a considerable section of the faithful broke away, and eventually separated itself, from the communion of the Universal Church. During these three centuries of separation, continuous efforts were made for re-establishing unity. However, until the beginning of this century, the results have been quite meagre.

The split and efforts for reunion

It was through the efforts of the Orthodox Metropolitan, Geevarghese Mar Ivanios, that an organized reunion movement finally started. The Metropolitan Mar Ivanios was an erudite person. He was the first Orthodox clergyman to obtain a postgraduate university degree and, as such, he was held in great respect by all. From his earliest days, he dedicated himself to God and to his service. With his intense loyalty to the Church and his unique achievements as a scholar and an administrator, he was promoted to highly responsible positions in the Church. With his keen mind and all-consuming love for Jesus Christ, the young priest looked far beyond the borders of his small Christian community. He realized, with great anguish, that the children of St Thomas had not faithfully continued the great mission entrusted to the Apostle by Jesus Christ. In his autobiography, Mar Ivanios has said: "It must be reckoned as a great crime that the Malankara Syrian Community, which claims origin from St Thomas the Apostle, and an antiquity of twenty centuries, has not so far done anything significant with regard to its mission and the purpose for which it was established. We must admit that the wonderful light that was kindled in AD 52, at the command of Our Saviour Jesus Christ, still remains in its initial stage; it has not shed its radiance, in the surrounding darkness."

He was fired by great enthusiasm and expressed his determination to take up and to continue this great mission. "It must be a great tragedy," he said, "if we do not make reparation for the past. If India remains in spiritual ignorance and has not embraced the faith, the Malankara Syrian Community will one day be held responsible for it. Whatever be the omissions and the lethargy of the past, the Malankara Syrian Community should now wake up and act in such a way that they make amends also for the negligence of the past. The all-important duty of the Christian Church is the proclamation of the Gospel."

Resigning from the position in the Orthodox Church, Fr Geevarghese went away to Bengal, the cultural capital of India, and there, taking up a teaching post in a Christian university, he began to plan for the future. He made as many contacts as possible with men of eminent positions in the various Christian communities and even outside. In consultation with them, and with their support, he started a programme of training young men and women for the service of evangelization.

Priests and evangelization

From the very beginning Fr Geevarghese understood the vital role of priests in evangelization and in the life of the Church and its entire ministry. "The spiritual growth of the priests," according to him, "is the same as the spiritual growth of the community. Schools and even seminaries are not so important as the ministry of the priests. Their mission is much more valuable and much more pleasing in the sight of God."

It is interesting to consider the reflections of the Metropolitan on priestly life, ideals and training. Since it was through his service and leadership that the Syro-Malankara Church eventually took shape, his earlier thoughts and ideals have a certain normative value for the Syro-Malankara Church in its present and future discipline. This is how the Metropolitan expressed himself: "The members of a missionary group should not be left to live and act according to the good pleasure of each one. There should be rules of conduct suitable to their ideal. If they are married people, they will not be able to carry out mission work vigorously. If they preach the Gospel like ordinary people, acting on their own, and without a rule of life, no purpose will be served and they will not be able *to gather the harvest in proportion to its abundance*. Missionary work is not to be done with words and statements; it must be performed through a virtuous life and genuine service and charitable activities. A virtuous life is more important than virtuous deeds. The conviction grew on me that to possess God is far more important than to serve God."

Monastic life – an attempt to revive missionary activities

Adopting the monastic life, according to the rule of St Basil, Fr Geevarghese spent long years in the seclusion of a mountainous area with a group of disciples. He and his companions prayed, reflected and waited for God's guidance. He also founded a monastery for women with an intense life of prayer and ascetic practices. They joined the monks in this search for Christian unity.

In the Orthodox Church, for many generations, missionary activities were almost nil. Temporal preoccupations and long drawn-out litigations for Church properties had almost totally absorbed the time and the energy of the clergy. There was very little pastoral ministry for the faithful. Spiritual life was at a very low ebb. The strong religious traditions in the Christian families, healthy personal relations among the spouses, regular prayers and the pious reading of the Word of God, kept the light of faith from fading out. This was the only silver lining in an otherwise dark atmosphere in the Orthodox Church.

Fr Geevarghese had left his native land for Bengal partly to have a respite from the tragic experiences in his Church. Things were worse when he returned. With a heart full of anguish, he began to think seriously about the future of the Church. Meanwhile, in the year 1925, Fr Geevarghese was ordained bishop with the name Mar Ivanios, and was given charge of the Religious Community of the Imitation of Christ, which he had started. This community had begun establishing churches in various eparchies with permission from the Malankara Metropolitan. In order not to become involved in the litigations, which were besetting the entire Jacobite Orthodox Church, these new churches were made independent of the general administration of the Orthodox Church. This was a far-sighted policy of Metropolitan Mar Ivanios.

Unity – the immediate concern of all

The prelate started consultations with a number of bishops, priests and lay leaders of his Church who shared his concerns. At this stage, it was not clear for them what ultimate form Christian unity would take. At one stage, there was even an idea of establishing relations with the Russian Orthodox Church. However, Mar Ivanios was eventually attracted towards the Catholic Church, and in this he was supported by several bishops, eminent priests and well-informed lay people. There was already a good number of priests and lay men who had preceded him into the communion of the Catholic Church. In fact, during the long years of separation, continuous efforts were being made to heal the wound. There were several occasions when corporate reunion seemed almost within reach, but through the vicissitudes of history, this noble objective eluded all except a few individuals and small groups. Some of these leading lay people whom the Metropolitan had consulted, proposed that it would be ideal to retain our ancient liturgical traditions with the system of administration of the Western Church, which had proved very helpful for the growth of Christian life, for missionary activities and in the entire service of the Church for the benefit of humanity.

The all-important Synod and its resolutions

A Synod of Bishops of the Orthodox Church was held in 1926 at Parumala, a sacred sanctuary of the Orthodox. In this synod, it was decided to seek formal union with the Catholic Church. Metropolitan Mar Ivanios was chosen by the synod to make necessary correspondence with the Holy See.

The following is the form of petition which was finally submitted to the Holy See:

The Holy Synod of the Catholicate prays that they be admitted into the unity of the Catholic Church, themselves
1. Preserving the ancient rites and rituals
2. Retaining for the Holy Synod, and for the individual bishops, their jurisdiction over all the Jacobite Syrians that come into reunion, and

3. Accepting the supremacy of the Holy See, the Pope being the successor of St Peter, the Chief of the Apostles of Our Lord.

A positive reply from Rome came after four long years. Meanwhile, due to various pressures and circumstances, the signatories of the petition for communion with the Catholic Church, with the exception of Metropolitan Mar Ivanios and Bishop Mar Theophilos, withdrew from their resolve. The Holy See in its reply accepted in substance the request of the petitioners. The longed-for reunion was thus effected in September 1930.

During these long negotiations, Mar Ivanios, among other things, had shown serious concern about the life and the discipline of priests. He made definite proposals for their continued training and spiritual formation.

Celibacy and the Malankara Catholic Church

Celibacy of priests was especially in Mar Ivanios' thoughts. The Holy See was generous and well-disposed to make necessary concessions, as in other cases of reunion of Oriental communities with the Catholic Church. The Metropolitan, solely concerned about the well-being and progress of his Christian community within the Catholic Church, deliberately opted for a celibate clergy for the future. In this, he had the support of the priests and the leading lay people, whose advice he sought. The Holy Father approved this choice, which had to be, and was, made once for all. This was the final decision from Rome:

The Holy See, on account of its special regard to the priests of Malankara, desires that those Malankarites, who come into the Catholic Church, should not lag behind the Malabar and Latin priests, in matters of great importance, like priestly celibacy. Therefore, it is hoped that the Malankarites will accept this way of life. But this will not stand in the way of married priests, who reunite themselves with the Catholic Church.

The deacons who were married could proceed to priestly ordination. In the case of subdeacons and those below them, in the clerical order, special permission is to be obtained in each case.

The wisdom of the choice of the Metropolitan, and the decision of the Holy See, has been amply justified by the results, as manifested in the life and growth of the Malankara Catholic Church ever since. The Church has grown numerically. From a handful of those who were reunited in 1930 (five in the first instance), in the course of 62years, there are over 300,000 faithful, and over 400 priests.

The fruitfulness of the Malankara Catholic Church, in the field of evangelization, is consoling and is in God's providence the continuing realization of the hopes and ideals of Archbishop Mar Ivanios for the children of St Thomas. There are today, under the three eparchies of the Syro-Malankara Church, 800 mission centres, all making steady progress. In addition, the number of priests of the Malankara Catholic Church serving outside the boundaries of the three eparchies is also quite considerable. There is every hope that this number will grow in the years to come. Again, the services rendered by the Malankara Catholic Church in the field of education, social welfare and in every field of human promotion are unparalleled in the history of the Malankara Syrian Church. This is evident from the appreciation and recognition of the general public and the State and Central Governments of India.

In India, among the Orientals separated from the Catholic Church, there has been no uniformity in the observance of priestly celibacy. However, bishops have always been celibate. It is certain that celibate priests existed among the Syrians before the schism took place and that such priests were held in great honour by the people. Moreover, remarriage was not allowed. Married priests, among the Orthodox, were to keep sexual abstinence during the period of celebrating the Holy Mysteries. Since in the Catholic Church daily celebration of the Holy Qurbana is customary, it is most appropriate, according to the sense of the faithful, that the Malankara Catholic priests practise perpetual abstinence.

Celibacy as the Indians see it

It seems quite appropriate here to recall the sensitivity of the people of India regarding celibacy in general and celibacy of priests in particular. In India, renunciation of worldly pleasures is the hallmark of a person of God. A celibate *Brahmachari* is one who lives and moves in *Brahman* (God). The great spiritual leader of modern India, Swami Vivekananda, said: "Without chastity, there can be no spiritual strength. The spiritual leaders of men have been very continent and this is what gave them power." Priestly celibacy is quite in keeping with the spiritual ethos of India. Mahatma Gandhi, whom Pope John Paul II acknowledged as "a symbol of the highest qualities and values of the Indian people, and is admired in every country of the world", said: "Celibacy is a great help, inasmuch as it enables one to lead a life of full surrender to God... Protestantism did many good things, but one of its few evils was that it ridiculed celibacy. It is celibacy that has kept Catholicism green up to the present day."

If the non-Christians do not fail to see the advantage of celibacy for the good of religion and society, for a Christian, however, the motives for celibacy are much more deep and the benefits are much more lofty. Jesus, who lived a virgin life and exhorted his close followers to leave all, including marriage and family attachments, is the ultimate inspiration and the most exalted model of perfect renunciation. "If any man comes to me without hating his father, mother, wife, children, brothers, sisters, yes, and his own life too, he cannot be my disciple" (Lk 14:26).

It is true that in the early Church, celibacy was not imposed as a necessary condition for discipleship, even upon those who were to enter the sacred ministry. However, the example and the words of Jesus Christ, as well as the fervent exhortation of St Paul, bring out the deep meaning and the spiritual advantages of celibacy. "I would like to see you free from all worry. An unmarried man can devote himself to the Lord's affairs, all he need worry about is pleasing the Lord; but a married man has to bother about the world's affairs and devote himself to pleasing his wife; he is torn two ways" (1 Cor 7:32-34).

The priest who is taken from among his people, and appointed for them, is to be the faithful and wise servant the Master has put in charge of his household to give them their food at the proper time. Jesus invites the disciple to remain in him so that, with the reciprocal presence of Jesus in him, he bears much fruit, fruit that will last.

An analogy from nature

Following the example of the Master, who illustrated his teachings with the ways of Providence in nature, we can draw a simple and useful analogy. In Psalm 19, we read about God sending out the sun to sustain life on this earth:

High above, he pitched a tent for the sun,
who comes out of his pavilion like a bridegroom
exulting like a hero to run his race.
He has his rising on the edge of heaven,
the end of his course is its furthest edge,
and nothing can escape his heat.

We know that, although all creatures are open to the heat and light of the sun, in the providence of God, only one of God's creatures (the humble plant) is the channel for communicating this life-giving energy to other living creatures.

Of the spiritual order, the prophet Malachi tells us: "But

145

for you, who fear my name, the Sun of Righteousness will shine out, with healing in its rays" (4:2). Jesus Christ, the Sun of Justice, is the source of all supernatural life and fruitfulness. It is through his priests, that he distributes his grace, the nourishment for supernatural life. The keys of the heavenly treasure house have been confidently handed over to them. It is manifest that the great High Priest is Christ himself. The fruitfulness of the minister will depend upon his intimacy with this High Priest – "if one remains in me and I in him..."

In nature, the more complete and the more unhindered the plant world is, in its openness and exposure to the sun and to its rays of light, the more abundant its vigour and its fruitfulness. In a similar way, the priest, who is the channel of divine light and life for God's children, the more complete and more unhindered his openness and exposure to Jesus, the more abundant will be his own spiritual vigour and his fruitfulness as a minister. Any cloud, or any shadow, that may come between the priest and the Master will in that measure lessen his effectiveness as a faithful and wise servant. The consecration of the priest to Christ, in a spousal relation, through the vow of chastity, is an inestimable grace and a help to him to turn to Jesus with singleness of purpose and to be wholly in him, so that he may bear much fruit and the fruit may remain.

Conclusion

In Asia, where two-thirds of humanity live, and where Catholics are less than 2%, the need for a fruitful apostolate is overwhelming. "The harvest is great, the labourers few." Every unit of energy, every moment of time, is required for the work most urgently and insistently asked of the priest by the Lord of the harvest. It is no time for looking back and brooding over the structures. Evangelization is not one issue among many, but the *"unum necessarium"*.

Celibacy: Fidelity to one's priestly identity

Dominic Tang Yee-ming

Archbishop of Canton

I was fourteen years old when I told my mother that I wished to be a priest. She sent me to Macau about 40 miles west of Hong Kong (where I was born) to enter St Joseph's seminary located there. Six years later, I obtained my bishop's permission to enter the Portuguese province of the Society of Jesus. After the usual studies, I was ordained in Shanghai in 1941 and remained in that city ministering to the Cantonese-speaking Catholics until I returned to Canton in 1946 and was assigned to Shekki, a city to the North of Macau. On 1 October 1950, Pius XII nominated me as Apostolic Administrator of the Canton Diocese.

These first years of priestly ministry were difficult ones, for the Communists were already in power and the Catholic faithful were undergoing intense pressures. My approach was pastoral and my first care was to animate the clergy who had been disheartened by the revolutionary changes that were then taking place in China – the Sino-Japanese War and following upon this the Communist take-over of power. I initiated a programme of intense pastoral activity with frequent sermons, retreats and other devotional practices. I invited the clergy and Sisters to take part in this ministry.

Relations with the political authorities deteriorated owing to my refusal to countenance the Patriotic Association they had set up to separate the Chinese Church from the Holy See. I myself was subjected to six public denunciations and finally arrested and brought to jail on 5 February 1958. For the following 22 years, I was kept isolated from all family and friends. During seven years, I was kept in solitary confinement even from my fellow prisoners. Prayer and the Spirit of the Lord sustained me especially in those dark hours when at times I felt far from the Lord.

It is from this background that I have reflected on the theme presented to me for comment: celibacy – the heart of a priest's identity and commitment. How do I view celibacy for the priest? I see it as a response to a call from the Lord, to give oneself totally to him and to the care of his people. A married man has obligations to his wife and family. These are of prime importance and he cannot shirk them without serious detriment to himself and his family. This is his responsibility before the Lord. For his way of life – the married state – is his response to the call of the Lord. If a priest were to be married, this commitment to family would take precedence over his pastoral ministry. Since this is so, I ask, how can a priest, who is called to dedicate himself totally to his people, marry? He would be immersed in his own world, concerned and preoccupied about his wife and children, and would be seriously torn between two polarities his family and the people to whom he ministers.

A priest's commitment is a response to a call from the Lord. The Lord himself did not marry. He gave himself totally to his people. It is in this way that the priest imitates the Lord. I realize that there are those in the Church today who find this type of celibate commitment difficult, some say even impossible. Perhaps we should learn a lesson from the Chinese Communists. During the Cultural Revolution in China, many of the clergy were forced into marriages. This was one way the Communists attacked the Church and its ministers. They did not understand celibacy, belittled it and wanted to do away with it. There were priests who got married. However, over the years, the Communists have come to realize that Catholics will not accept these married priests as their ministers. They strongly oppose having any Catholic priest who is married to act as their spiritual leader. I do not believe that they are passing personal judgement on these priests, but what they are saying, it seems to me, is that they want celibate priests who can dedicate their whole lives to the Lord and to his people. No other commitment will do. I witnessed many cases of infidelity to celibacy in my long years of pastoral service. It is not to make any judgement on the persons involved, but it is sad to say that most of them did not remain faithful to their Christian life. Some wanted to convert but they were hindered by their 'wives' and not a few even lost their faith in the end. I cite two examples that are common knowledge in China. In Shanghai, a married priest wanted to say Mass in the church. The Catholics would not permit him to do this and took him off the altar. In Kunming, a bishop got married and was going to say a public Mass. Local Catholics heard of this and publicly advertised the fact. The bishop did not say Mass. This opposition coming from the Catholic community has forced the Communist authorities to change their policy. This is not easy for them to do. They have had to admit that only unmarried priests can be ordained to serve these communities. They do this not out of any admiration of the celibate state as such but to preserve harmony in the communities.

Does this demand of Chinese Catholic communities for celibate priests rest solely on traditional practices? This is to say, do these communities wish to have celibate priests only because that was what was done in the past and therefore should continue for the future? I believe not. I believe that the reasons behind these Catholic communities demanding celibate priests goes much deeper than mere tradition, although this may be one of the factors involved. Celibacy for the kingdom of God has its own value as the Lord himself states. St Paul counsels celibacy. One of its values he sees is the freedom it gives to the person. Celibates enjoy their freedom as a special gift by which they can fully dedicate themselves to the Lord and to his work. This sets such persons apart. This does not mean that these people are better than others who follow a different calling from the Lord. What it does mean is that the celibate person is set apart for total service to the Christian community. This is, I believe and as my experience teaches me, one of the chief reasons why our Chinese Catholic communities demand celibacy for their spiritual leaders. They want to have a person dedicated and determined to follow the Lord completely and who will in turn lead them to know, love and follow him. They themselves realize that they have many concerns and occupations. Owing to these concerns, they may not always have clear insight into the ways of the Lord. They trust their spiritual leaders who have completely dedicated themselves to the Lord, to help them discover his ways in their lives.

Celibacy is not something completely foreign to our Chinese culture. Buddhist monks and nuns do not marry. They are seeking liberation from desire, a detachment from worldly pleasures that may impede them from attaining Nirvana. In the eyes of the Buddhist faithful, monks and nuns are expected to be faithful to their vows. They should not marry and if they do the Buddhist faithful would prefer them to return to the world rather than continue being a 'married monk or nun'. I note this fact not because I wish to identify the Buddhist motivation for celibacy with the Christian profession of celibacy undertaken from the kingdom of God as proclaimed by Jesus in the Gospel. I just wish to emphasize the value placed upon celibacy, and the expectations even non-Catholics have for fidelity in living such vows. As in the case of Catholic priests, the Communist authorities have been compelled to recognize this fact and so they have ceased forcing Buddhist monks and nuns to marry.

I have personally witnessed many times over the inner strength the Lord gives to a person facing the loss of freedom, suffering and even death. Specifically, I wish to talk about those who have vowed celibacy and who have persevered in their commitment. I am well aware that not only celibate Christians have had to witness to Christ. The Annals of the Chinese martyrs, once it is written, will be long with the names of the lay persons, men and women, young and old, who along with priests and sisters have had to endure suffering, imprisonment and even death for their commitment to the Lord. I wish to point out that a celibate life, one that is lived in close union with the Lord, does prepare one very well for the supreme sacrifice of one's life if this is the path that the Lord leads his faithful disciple to follow.

There was my secretary, Fr Anthony Ngan Tak-Kang. Many called him a living saint. He would have smiled at this title and be amazed that his very ordinary life would merit such acclamation. He would refuse such praise and would continue to carry out his daily duties and live his life in accord with the promise he had made to the Lord many years before. He would see nothing heroic in this. However, when the moment of testing did arrive, he showed more than ordinary courage and fortitude. His outstanding example is but one among many that his brother priests from all over China have given and who had to undergo the same crucible of suffering. In his relations with women, Fr Ngan was always courteous and reserved. This did not prevent him from performing his pastoral work for whoever requested it, men or women. No one ever suggested that he was unfaithful in the smallest degree in his obligations to priestly celibacy. This is one of the main reasons why he was so respected and even venerated by all the Catholics who knew him.

He was a very good secretary. He understood my mind well and was an excellent advisor especially helping me make the many hard decisions during those difficult days when the Communists were applying more and more pressure to the Church. On one occasion, we were trying to find the means of paying the heavy taxes the authorities were imposing upon us. At the same time, we had to support our clergy and the sisters. Some counselled the selling of Church property and possessions. He simply said no; we could not dispose of Church property in violation of canon law, even if this meant that we had to live a poor life and suffer any privations. He wished that we walk with the poor Christ and preserve Church property. Certainly the pride of possessions did not motivate him. He just wanted to make sure that the Church had the means and wherewithal to continue its mission in the future when more difficult days were to come. A few months later we did lose all Church property. It was confiscated by the so-called 'Real Estate Management Committee' – cadres of the Communist government and members of the Patriotic Association comprised this committee. In no way does this change the correctness of Fr Anthony's advice given at a time when good men and women were hard put to see beyond present travails.

He was arrested on the same day as I was and, like myself, was imprisoned without trial. He was sent to a labour camp in the North of Guangdong province. All that he owned at the time were the few rags on his back. He had always lived poorly and was constantly giving things away to those poorer than himself. Coarse food, hard labour and illness – his legs became infected and swollen so that he could not walk – caused his death. He never once wavered in his commitment to the Lord and fidelity to the Church.

I could go on to mention other priests as well, men such as my vicar general, Fr Andrew Chan Jik-san who took my place when I was arrested. He was brought to Beijing and pressured to become a bishop in my stead by joining the Patriotic Association under government control. He always refused. Back in Canton he was arrested. Beaten and kept in a police station, he was able to sneak out and crawled home on all fours. Some Christians took him in and he died soon after.

There were many more such witnesses to the faith in China. The words of the Letter to the Hebrews come to mind and they encourage us who are left behind: "Let us persevere in running the face that lies before us, while keeping our eyes fixed on Jesus" (12:1).

Just before I was released from prison, I underwent a final examination. I was questioned on my attitude towards the Vatican, I answered: "I am a Catholic and I cannot separate from the Pope." This angered the official. "After 22 years you are still the same stubborn old man." Ten days later he came back to me and said: "First of all, you are honest. You have never used money given to the Church for your own personal benefit, not even the money given to you by your mother. Second, you never played around with women and, finally, you never have harmed the people." These were the three reasons given for my release. "Never playing around with women" was the negative way that official used to attest to the fact that I had kept my celibacy intact. Of course, this was a grace of the Lord. It was a grace even manifest to an atheistic government that had no use for celibacy. Yet in releasing me from prison and inducing this as one of the reasons, they were forced to admit that something about celibacy was good. They could not say why, but we Christians can, for it is Jesus who said: "Some have renounced marriage for the sake of the kingdom of heaven. Whoever can accept this ought to accept it" (Mt 19:12, New American Bible).

Celibacy: the view of a Zen monk from Japan

Soko Morinaga

Buddist monk. Rector of Hanazono University

Examples of the marriage of monks in Japan can be found as early as the Heian period (794-1185). Moreover, beginning from the time of Shinran (1173-1262) and Ippen (1239-1289), who were known as *hijiri*, or wandering mendicants, there are many examples of the marriage of monks during the Kamakura (1185-1333), Muromachi (1336-1570), and Edo periods (1600-1867). So from the point of view of ordinary Japanese people, the marriage of monks was not regarded as something out of the ordinary.

An edict, number 133, issued by the new Meiji government in 1872 ordered that monks should be free to "eat meat, take wives, and shave their heads" as they chose. From that time, the secularization of monks proceeded rapidly. In Taisho in 1920 the Jodo (Pure Land) School of Buddhism issued a set of Regulations for Temple Families. From this time, the treatment of temple families became an important issue. In this way, the marriage of monks, instead of being viewed as a question of doctrine or the precepts of monastic life, came to be taken up as a problem of personal attraction of temple management, or as a matter affecting the lives of temple families. The problem, then, became less a strictly religious one, and more a matter of how to deal with the inheritance of temple headships and the social status, rights, and property of temple families.

The issue of monastic celibacy differs for each sect of Japanese Buddhism and for each individual monk. We cannot say that the social issues I have outlined above reflect the definitive state of contemporary Japanese Buddhism but it is true that where these various problems do exist, they arise from the marriage of monks. Moreover, in thinking about this question, we should not overlook the fact that nuns are usually neglected and that an exclusively male-centred point of view is argued.

In this brief essay, however, I would like to discuss the issue of monastic celibacy not from this social angle, but from the personal point of view of my own religious experiences as a Zen monk, and on the basis of 'faith', in terms of Zen teaching and the monastic precepts.

What is essential for the Buddhist is the self-awakening of and to the 'three treasures': the Buddha, the Dharma, and the Sangha community. Rather than being an object of faith in the context of a lord-servant relationship such as that of a creator and the ones that are saved, *Buddha* designates that which lets exist everything that is. In Zen, this is also called 'One Mind' or 'Buddha-nature'. *Dharma* signifies the matrix of impermanence and cause-effect in which Buddha as a phenomenon ceaselessly undergoes creation, change, birth and death. Finally, *sangha* denotes the subtle order and harmony among the phenomena. Thus, with the self-awakening of and to reality as it truly is – which is expressed by the term 'three treasures' – it becomes clear that all existence is originally without any subjective 'I' and without any object an 'I' could possess. However, in terms of public life, *sangha* also designates a group of Buddhists whose members attempt to transmit by their own self-awakening the very Buddha-nature which the Buddha awakened to.

A person who wants to become a monk or nun must go through a specific process. In the initial ordination ceremony, the precepts are accepted. As a condition for this acceptance of the precepts, one must first express one's resolve to leave one's home which forms a root of attachment. Furthermore, one must be more than 20 years of age, and it is absolutely required that one's parents approve one's leaving home. Thus a monk or nun is, as a member of the *sangha*, a person who has left his or her home[1] and is either celibate from the outset or becomes celibate upon entering monastic life. This is also a practical expression of one's faith in the three treasures (no 'I', and no object).

While the establishment of religious faith is, needless to say, a very personal and internal event, the social status of 'monk' or 'nun' presupposes a monastic community called *sangha*. Both from the point of view of the establishment of one's own faith and from that of a harmonious effort in the *sangha* community to help each other towards self-awakening, the monks' and nuns' lack of possessions is an essential condition.

Although the inner effort to deepen the 'faith' in one's heart and the altruistic effort to help others to attain religious peace of mind are in essence just two sides of one coin, one must recognize that historically, in the monastic community (*sangha*), the former endeavour did not necessarily form a unity with the altruistic effort that aims at saving members of the secular society.

In Southeast Asian Buddhism, the monastic community is still central; in contrast, the various forms of Mahayana Buddhism in China and Japan tend towards secularism. In the trend of historical secularization of modern civilisation throughout the world, one may in Japan sometimes have trouble speaking to communities of home-leavers. Nevertheless, and in spite of the limited number of such vocations, I can say as one member of the Japanese Buddhist *sangha* that in this day and age there are in fact still Zen monks and nuns who consciously choose to remain celibate for life.

With regard to the corpus of scriptures on monastic precepts, one finds that the history of the institutionalization of monastic precepts can also be called a history of the breaking of these rules. The repeated addition of more detailed rules was necessary precisely because the precepts were broken, and it served to prevent just that. Paradoxically, the attempt to kill off desires and attachments inside the monastic community by way of precepts, produced more evil ways of breaking these precepts; and while sight was lost of the gist of the teaching, superficial hypocrisy and self-righteous interpretations became rampant.

The Buddhist monk Saichô (767-822) dared to abrogate the multitude of traditional small precepts in favour of the sole precept to "awaken to the fundamental one-mind of Mahayana". He established a ceremony for the taking of this precept and built a Mahayana ordination platform for the purpose on Mount Hiei near Kyoto. Since then, various branches of Japanese Buddhism have adhered to this. But Zen, following in the steps of its Chinese tradition, upheld an original structure of mutual complementarity of the monastic and secular communities and thus did not completely give way to lay Buddhism. Although this was a contradictory compromise of a kind that is again different from that of Southeast Asian Buddhism, one can say that the realization of this kind of contradiction bears potential for the future. However, it also proved to be a cause for confusion in monastic Japanese Buddhism.

At any rate, the specific character of Japanese Buddhism, formed through the abolition of the small precepts in favour of the Precept of Mahayana One-Mind and the view that both personal and altruistic practice appear naturally, is an active response to the problems of secular society. Wanting to contribute to world peace and well-being, Japanese Buddhism shows an increasingly strong tendency to this worldly benefit. At the same time, it acquires more and more the character of a lay community rather than that of a monastic one. In particular, the a-religious tendency of modern civilization – and along with it the loss of family ethics, the contempt for life, and the anthropocentric resources and world-wide destruction of the environment – has led to an extreme situation which ultimately can not be dealt with in terms of superficial this-worldly profit thinking. It is true that the home-leavers, too, tend to strive more for secular fortune than for the faith arising from the self-awakening of the three treasures. They view the monastic community that ought to be their basis lightly and disregard its rules, and they are drawn into the secular world with a household and private property before having finished their own spiritual quest.

If I may relate here my personal experience: After leaving home and being ordained, I spent a period of 20 years (from age 20 to age 40) in personal practice to establish that faith which is called *satori*. Since then I have been involved in practices to benefit others in the secular world, and celibacy has always seemed most natural to me. I do not feel at all constrained by the precepts and have not felt any grave hindrance due to desire. Ever since I became a monk, the faith in connection with the self-awakening of the three treasures and the abstinence from personal possessions has seemed natural to me. I think that my way of being a Zen monk would have long ago come to a dead end if I had had to uphold by force a voluntary precept or a related threat of punishment for these two conditions for being a religious person: faith on the inside, and a life without material possessions on the outside.

When the Japanese Buddhist Saint Hônen (1133-1212) was asked whether a Buddhist religious person should be celibate or not, he said: "If it is easier for him or her to express faith by reciting the Buddha's name alone, he or she should be celibate. If it is easier to do that with a spouse, it is better to marry. What is important is only how one expresses one's faith in reciting the Buddha's name."

The establishment of religious faith cannot but be personal, and in this sense I fully agree with Hônen. However, as a Zen monk who has entered a monastic community in order to accomplish both personal religious practice and help for others, I feel that it was easier to do this without a family and the ensuing necessity to have personal property; so for me the choice of celibacy and poverty was a natural and joyful one. I certainly am not the only person who feels joy about celibate life; already in the old Theravada Buddhist tradition of Southeast Asia one finds many poems that sing of the joy of celibacy. Although there may be desires such as sexual desires, this joy protects celibate life.

It is rather difficult to speak of both the views held in the history of Buddhism and my personal experience in just a few pages, but in conclusion I would like to emphasize that the life of a true religious person does not ban desire by inner will power or by outer pressure. Rather, it is due to a natural manifestation of Buddha-mind that life without possessions becomes a joy accompanying both activities for one's own benefit and activity for the benefit of others.

Since the majority of the monks and nuns that constitute the *sangha* have not yet realized this, inner effort of will and vows and outer rules become necessary. Wherever there is coercion to conform to such rules, be it from the inside or the outside, there is bound to be hypocrisy and transgression. From a historical point of view, too, it is clear how meaningless it is to try to eradicate this contradiction by systematic reform. There is only one way to completely transcend this contradiction, and that is by the joy of the monk's and nun's own self-awakened faith. If they ignore this joy of faith and attempt to preserve a *sangha* that relies on some system, the *sangha* will surely at some point perish. But even if that kind of *sangha* perishes, the three treasures will not perish. Just as the green leaves of spring sprout after the autumn leaves have been burnt, the Buddha *dharma* will with certainty appear anew in a different form.

NOTE

1. 'Leaving home' is the literal rendering of the Sino-Japanese expression used when someone enters a Buddhist monastery.

Priestly celibacy: Misogyny of the Catholic Church?

Maria Adelaide Raschini

Professor of Theoretical Philosophy at the University of Genoa

That priestly celibacy can be associated with a presumed misogyny characterizing the Catholic Church is merely one corollary of commonly held ideas that make a few preliminary reflections necessary in this essay. Besides, with the prevalence of a mentality alien to the Christian spirit, questions can arise which many Christians too come to find disturbing, acting as they frequently do as inner gadflies. Often enough, under the guise of 'necessity', these questions barely conceal an underlying inconsistency or spiritual weakness making their sophistical nature and often ambiguous, marginal character readily recognizable to the alert Christian conscience. The Christian conscience should never allow itself to be disturbed by them, yet has a duty to take note of them lest an untimely silence, especially if misinterpreted, become accomplice to the infliction of even deeper wounds.[1]

It is timely to know what the world's intentions are

The argument over the celibacy of the Catholic priest is a typical example of those questions raised from time to time *sub specie boni*. A question of this particular type normally brings other, collateral ones along with it, such as the priesthood of women, their role within ecclesial society etc., and finally takes the form of a weird insinuation that one of the reasons for the celibacy of the Catholic priest is to be sought in the Church's real hostility to the female sex:

160

which would immediately lend plausibility and 'critical' honesty to the question of the Church's 'misogyny' as such.

We cannot, however, conceal the fact that the historical health of Christianity, generally speaking, does not seem to have been robust enough to consent to answer the aforesaid problems in a 'naturally Christian' way. The temptation to hearken to the voice of the world itself inasmuch as it is 'the world-voice', is so strong, so beguiling and so wide-spread, that we can never be too thoughtful or too wary. Not without agitation therefore, we approach this type of thinking, requiring a staunch heart, a mind fervently at-tached to the truth, a will directed to what is right: requir-ing, that is to say, that total disposition which, with God's grace, summons all our human powers together and con-sents to their being grafted on to the tree of life, by which I mean Christ. Divided, these powers risk failure even of their individual purposes: in 'fragmented' human nature, the intellect 'does not see', the will is 'passive', the heart disintegrates in 'indifference' which is, in short, exclusive love of self. Of such 'dividedness' meanwhile, the ques-tions behind which the modern mind masks its having chosen to become 'worldly' are a peculiarly appropriate sign. For it lives on a diet of rich and radical immanentism which sustains its culture and dominates its thinking, the latter accepting in passive and superficial manner not a few worn-out old commonplaces which it hails as acquisitions of truth. For an immanentism carried to extremes has in-deed flung wide the doors to the spirit of the world, and this – so disguised as to deceive – quickly becomes apparent once underlying *hybris* grows so strong that it strips off all disguise.

The curse of 'spiritual empiricism'

The most typical and most refined disguise adopted by the spirit of the world is one that assumes the likeness of a cultural *paideia,* and hence uses all the instruments of psychological persuasion in an effort to convince intelligent people. This makes 'historically' invalid the attitude of anyone who, even in connection with certain questions raised *a parte mundi* – and especially in the vain hope of better interpreting what is going on today – *would seek to undervalue the importance of intellectual training, as though spiritual maturity could leave this out of account.* A false argument, winning a sympathetic hearing even from the best intentioned of Christians precisely because it 'distracts' attention from the 'whole' (which is always the main issue), by inducing us to concentrate on details which in themselves are not devoid of plausibility. And since the human soul, being made for the truth, is always drawn to where it spies even a modicum of truth, the deceit finds sufficient room to worm its way in and seize on souls in good faith, precisely because *sub specie boni.* But this is the very essence of the temptation. Hence the need to be aware of the intrinsically falsifying procedures typical of the spirit of the world and to tackle them fairly and squarely. Hence the need to trust robustly in the weapon of reason wherever it can be used and to arouse ourselves once more to the responsibility of historical awareness, even as to questions which – such as that of priestly celibacy – seem only, or mainly, to concern the religious sphere.

The Fathers of the Church, who experienced and lived through periods of dramatic harshness, have left us a precious inheritance here. The Christian must never cease, by the light of revelation, to reason and think with that *fides quaerens intellectum,* lack of which in the contemporary world has assented to and often nourished areas of irrationality and unquestionably has encouraged the spread of that 'spiritual empiricism' afflicting the modern world, some of Christianity not excluded. If we do not take note of the sophisms repeatedly advanced as arguments, and if we do not succeed in utterly piercing their disguise, any discourse runs the risk of failing since it cannot lead to 'entire' persuasion. More than ever today, the paganizing pressures

of the world require of the Christian an 'entire' training of
the spirit, an achievement of the synthesis of our powers,
with which we are called on to unite and strengthen one
another in conscious love.

Pagan mask and Christian countenance: spirit of transgression and spirit of obedience. The sophism of 'liberation'

Now, it is impossible to deal with any question put in
terms of historical expediency without knowing what conditions give rise to it. To understand instances passed off as
necessities of the moral, human, functional order, we must
first ask what it is in fact that dictates their being advanced.
Whence the need to identify the particular sophism of
contemporary 'de-formation' or *dys-paidagoghia*, where
the conditions of any possible transgression or, better, of
transgression as such, are concealed, understood as a 'sign'
of 'liberation from' and of 'self-affirmation'.

The sophism is always brought into play at the level of
principle, after paradoxically the theory has been advanced
that it would be 'wrong to raise matters of principle' on the
grounds that they are 'abstract'. Thus the sophism on which
all possible transgressions depend, is hidden where one
would be least likely to look for it, namely, in the appeal to
the intrinsically moral character of existence as such, that
is to say, to the principle of the 'goodness' of all that is.
The disguise has the apparent function of affirming and
clinching the principle of the goodness of existence; in fact
it uses it sophistically, in accordance with what we might
define as the most radical ontological transgression. Thus,
the sophism is cunningly and quickly prepared: if the Christian conception of reality entails the affirmation that all that
'is' is good, the sophism in its intrinsically deceitful way
insinuates: my 'natural desires' are legitimate from the fact
of existing and of being irresistible; therefore their demands and the things done in consequence are 'naturally'

good, since they cannot be expunged from the sphere of the goodness of existence other than at the price of infringing the rights of the subject in whom they inhere. Unwillingness to see this sophism for what it is – and the 'naturalism' of which is obvious – means having already so far abandoned the Christian spirit as to accept the postulate actually generating the sophism, as already to deny, rather than reinforce, the very truth that the sophism is designed to refute.

But this very 'unwillingness to see' has created the conditions, making room for this radical 'disorder', thanks to which historical physiology in one part of Christendom too is now on its deathbed: as is clear from the amount of evidence today as paganism makes its come-back. So grave a disturbance and disorder cannot but have causes to match. It will not be hard for us to identify them and, in doing so, we shall confirm the abyssal quality of the divergence between the Christian and the pagan spirits. A divergence which Rosmini helps us to measure thus: the Christian spirit, in recognizing its own weakness, errors and shortcomings, sees in the Truth the guiding norm for its growth as an intelligent, free entity and places the conditions for its own complete 'fulfilment' in *'freedom' from evil*. The pagan spirit on the other hand makes its own weaknesses the theoretical unit of measure and the criterion of 'ethical' approval, whence one becomes enslaved to them in the name of a false *'liberation' from the norm. Liberation from the norm* always leads to denial of the truth, to which pertains all that participates in the act of being and from which only the will-to-reject escapes. As a result we see the 'natural' and 'worldly' *koinonia*, and indeed complicity, between those who reject the truth out of egotistical love of self (*'practical' denial*: truth 'orders' the space of the subjective and hence discourages the free range of the passions) and those for whom the lawfulness of the subjective and of all its operations follows from their having rejected the notion of the truth (*'theoretical' denial*).

The responsibility of those who 'take advantage' of

these sophisms is truly enormous, since they go beyond the individual sphere and involve the fate of other people, who, however, are not regarded as 'neighbour'; for it is not given to all to see this and protect themselves from it. But those who do not detect the artfulness of the disguise cannot be held to blame. Saying as much does not necessitate or justify procedures on account of their underlying intentions. Rather, it means recognizing operations which, precise postulates having been accepted, follow on by inexorable logic: even were the postulate such as to negate all logic.

Now, the postulate of denial, be it theoretical or practical, becomes visible, thanks to the depressing evidence of its 'negatory' nature, at the level of its consequences, which can no longer be justified owing to the deceitful substitution of principle. So the radical and squalid spiritual lie has to be disguised: which refuses to distinguish between two antithetical attitudes – on the one hand, the fall through human weakness, where understanding is needed and love is due, and on the other, the rejection by the intellect and will of their proper ends, *viz* the true and the good, by virtue of which limpidity, sincerity and exactitude are enjoined. The fall through weakness needs the love that raises up again and sustains, that 'delivers from evil'; the rejectionist will is 'the will that divides the truth' (*dià-ballein*), a self-blinding which 'enjoins' all falls as 'liberation' from the truth.

Apparent ingenuousness and prejudices

If, therefore, a query is put 'historically' in the form: 'Is priestly celibacy perhaps the effect of misogyny on the part of the Catholic Church?', the question is only apparently 'ingenuous', since it can only have been framed in the course of a preceding mental journey which, precise premises having been accepted, can only arrive at attitudes which completely distort Christian truth and ecclesial reality. Hence the question can only be advanced once the misogyny of the Church is already taken for granted. Besides, therefore, not being 'ingenuous', the question is in no sense 'critical' either.

This has to be said straightaway, not only as regards the problem of women and the role accorded them in the Church (to which the question of the Church's presumed misogyny must bring us back), but almost all the captious questions to which people have recourse, almost as though it were a conscientious duty, whenever the topic of priestly celibacy comes up. Today's mental trickery, for the most part, runs as follows: the urgent need for a wider understanding among people, the need for an 'ecumenical' broadening of the sphere of 'the religious', the postulate of a 'planetary' catechesis (with consequent 'opening' for an increase in priestly vocations), must pass by way of a 'justification' of the human as such, given that this appears to be the only common denominator among people. Therefore, while Christian doctrine 'bases' the essence and dignity of the human on the intimately theistic constitution of the person and on awareness of our *religatio* to God, the spirit of the world, under guise of religiousness, smuggles in a relationship which – in the various modalities of spiritual empiricism spreading into the Christian sector too – in every way clinches the assumption of the self-sufficiency of human 'naturalness' which, along with the veritative basis of the idea of God, also drives out the notions of authority and discipline which depend on it. This inversion of values has led a part of the Christian world first to accept the historic-naturalistic thesis according to which God is no more than a human projection; and next, internally and logically has led from 'becoming aware' of the fictitious nature of the 'projection' to denying any plausibility in the idea at all.

All *religatio ad Deum* as ontological relationship being thus cut off, what remains of the human personality is the range of feelings that can be experienced 'as regards' a human being whose 'justification' lies in his or her own 'naturalness': *a human being 'too human' because no more than human,* owing to a methodical reduction of his or her theistically oriented 'nature', which is then his human nature.

The journey, however succinctly thus described, is really a road that needs to be travelled backwards until we touch the roots of the aforementioned problem and decipher its various aspects, in which even serious questions risk being compressed and distorted. Let it be said in passing: responsibility for assuming the duty of being historically and critically aware, grows greater in Catholic culture day by day.

The radical denial is reflected in matters concerning order and obedience

It is not a sign of Christian love to assent in a disordered fashion to solicitations, be they what they may, merely adducing in excuse that they concern the so-called 'secondary Christianity', namely, that part of or in Christianity not constituting a dogmatic element. What is not a dogmatic element, for this very reason, neither nourishes 'theological' anxieties in the Christianly orientated conscience nor does it injure the firmness of faith.

It may well happen that we find ourselves having to live in difficult situations implying disciplinary obedience though not, as such, involving a matter of dogma. But this difficulty 'does not make law' except in relation to that awareness of the law which we have chosen to obey in response to a precise vocation: that law inclusive of all obediences since founded on the obedience of Christ, who came to do the Father's will. This means that the spirit of obedience in the widest and most positive sense inheres in the essence of the priestly vocation and even dictates those acts of self-denial, those life-styles, those relationships which otherwise it would be for us ourselves to 'regulate' in accordance with other, different vocational choices during our lives. In a certain measure, an analogy may be drawn with another sacrament, marriage: the strict and imperishable tie established between husband and wife makes them 'positively' choose and accept everything which, internally, would be suffered 'negatively' if, *ab initio,* it were received according to provisional, unstable and temporary modalities. This, therefore, refers us on to the problem of 'vocation' and the serious and essential responsibility for training each of us for our own vocation, and makes the care taken by the Church in the screening and process of 'advanced training' of its priests all the more valuable.

Vocations and vocation

Many and diverse are the ways, all ordered if directed towards Being; within the horizon of the existence in which we exist, each of us, being aware that life is a 'time of trial', ought to find – and should be helped to find – the way on which we are 'called' to undergo 'our particular' trial. Each way involves 'total' commitment, even when we are talking of vocations other than that of the priesthood. How much the more radical, therefore, will the commitment of priestly vocation be, if the Church has given clear signs constantly maintaining esteem for the 'non-separation' of the 'two charisms' of priestly vocation and celibacy? It is not a matter concerning the greater or lesser 'functionality' of a 'status' (i.e., married or single), but rather of the *intrinsic congruity* thanks to which the total gift particularly required by any vocation which truly is one, becomes absolute.

We should emphasize that a *dilemma of conscience* is one thing (a position from which the individual's conscience cannot escape by recourse to a spiritual guide, by whom, moreover, the conscience is thrown back on the confirming of its own will of free acceptance); and to theorise that the dilemma of conscience, whatever it may be, may become an occasion for reformulating the law is another. Faced with the superficial spread of approval for this latter theory, faced with a reformulation of thought, richer in presumption than in charity, that an individual choice (not yet freedom, which is always and only freedom for goodness and truth, that is to say, freedom from evil) may obtain and forthwith codify in priestly obedience, it only remains for us to come to a conclusion, not yet about the priesthood but about the – undeniable and now never mentioned – frailty of an individual who, even when consecrated, might think to make the total gift of himself to God even greater and more effective by sharing that love with another creature.

Nothing concerning life's contingencies can affect the exceptional nature of the priestly character: the priesthood remains intact in its exalted dignity, beyond human reach since established by Christ himself through the link with his Body and Blood, entrusted to the priest and only the priest to administer: "This dignity, which the angels do not have, I have given to man and especially to those whom I have chosen to be my ministers, considering them to be like angels... Of every soul I ask purity and charity, with love for me and for his neighbour... *But I ask greater purity of my ministers and more love for me and for their neighbour*, since they administer the Body and Blood of my only-begotten Son with ardour of charity and thirst for the salvation of souls, to the glory and praise of my name." Thus spake Truth to Catherine of Siena, a woman of immeasurable holiness and a Doctor of the Church. The gift of the priest's love to God is intrinsically weighted with a greater privilege, relating not to the priest's own degree of holiness but to the constituent character of the priesthood and its supreme, unrivalled dignity. Indeed, the greater number of interventions at the 1990 Synod of Bishops hinged on the priestly dignity as that which stems from divine election.

Undeniably, then, the Christian conscience, even in a priest, can experience situations of inner conflict. But existential situations do not make law, whereas the law, to be just, should foresee ways for solving the problematic situations which may arise. In this sense, not even merely human law, with the large measure of the conventional and the feasible that it inevitably contains, ought to contravene the principles of higher justice which confer legal substance on it: for the 'justification' of human law is its tendency and its capacity to satisfy the notion of justice that human beings hold in civil society and which, therefore, civil society cannot disappoint except at the cost of denying the very root of justice. This becomes a thousand times clearer when a law comes about and is imposed in the Church, not as a matter of human prudence but because inspired by the truth which is Christ, in whom justice and love are the same; since in *the Church every law pays homage to the law of Truth, Justice and Love, of which it is intended to be both expression and witness.*

If therefore human law-codes can invoke – as frequently they do – the criterion of the 'lesser evil' in order to mete out the 'least imperfect justice possible', the Church is by no means inspired by this criterion, but rather by the principle of 'the greatest good'. In this case, the perfect chastity and purity of the total gift of self correspond to the principle of 'the greatest good', the only one capable of reassembling within itself the multiple riches of human relationships and raising them to the forms required by the lofty dignity of the priesthood. And this certainly does not exclude friendship, esteem and the attitude of trust that a priest may also encourage to the benefit of the female members of his flock. The priest is a father to all, precisely because he has no wife and is, therefore, free of those primary duties which would bind him to the woman who became his wife and to those who would be his children according to the flesh. He is wedded to the Church of Christ, in whose mystical life every creature has its place beyond all generic differences; all creatures are truly equal in his sight, identical objects of his physical, spiritual and intellectual, loving care.

The 'Christian' woman and the priest

A preamble on love and women seems fitting here. Anyone who denied that love were the most rigorous and arduous of ties would evidently not be talking about love but would be putting themselves exclusively in the position of someone who expects (egoism) and not of someone who gives 'charity', and thus attributing to love the characteristics of the world's inclinations and emotions. Love is always an image of the Crucifixion, which is the loftiest expression thereof; it asks without ever setting limits to its most rigorous demands, grants no respite, does not admit indolence, rejects inertia. Just because it is so rigorous and demanding, love becomes the sweetest of ties, savoury nourishment of spirits, supreme solace of souls in the hardships of life.

The strong, very loving rigour of charity, since such it is, demands that the Christian conscience not frustrate its own spiritual energies by taking something precious away from them in the very 'time of trial'. Because of this, love submits its own dilemmas to sustained analysis by the strict yet also enlightened will, protected by prayer and by that providential trust which is the radical spirit of obedience. Much will be stripped away of what distresses us in the way of subjective perturbation, and only a little while spent in patience will be enough to make us realize how much of the inessential can be concealed in the most 'natural' of demands, that is to say, in that 'apparently' most 'justified'.

So how are we to deal, within the rigorous demand of all divine love which rejects indifference, with the question of the Church's 'misogyny', which is claimed to be one reason for the discipline of priestly celibacy? Put thus, we would have to say what we have here is a false problem and grossly formulated at that. Its grossness is so absolutely obvious: to accept even a partial formulation of it would be equivalent to maintaining that any request for one thing must always be motivated by the rejection of something else. In the vocation oriented towards Being, no choice occurs 'by exclusion' or, which is the same thing, no choice of whatever is true or whatever is good is made according to the criterion of the 'lesser evil'. Not every decision as such is denial; not at least within a Christian view of existence. Because this is so, a man does not take a wife and a woman does not take a husband *because*, among the possible choices, that woman or that man represents the 'lesser evil': but rather by positive 'election' of an indispensable personal relationship. And precisely because it consists in this positive election of the 'indispensable' person, the tie (the marital one) can be raised to the dignity of a sacrament, when it might otherwise appear only 'too human' and hence be exposed, among other things, to the risk of a pernicious insecurity: for it would rest on an entirely subjective base which would 'void' the marriage tie of content.

This somewhat general reflection will serve to introduce a few thoughts more to the point. If marriage is, as by its nature it is, a tie which comes into being on the basis of 'election' of the person with whom *to grow together* in Being, this stands in evident harmony with the disciplinary dictates of the Church, whether in relation to the sacrament of marriage or in relation to the sacrament of Order, or as regards what is of mutual concern to them. For, (1) it suppresses the plausibility of the theory of the presumed misogyny with which the Church is sometimes reproached on the basis of a selective use of certain passages in St Paul; (2) it furnishes a valuable criterion by which women can sort out their proper position in the ecclesial community and, in the light of Christian history, assess the degree of dignity with which the Church has crowned them; (3) it calls on the Church – particularly today – to make sure that the necessary and sufficient conditions of marriages be safeguarded when celebrated in a Catholic environment; (4) it contains the clearest indication of the fittingness of the union between the priestly and celibate states. A few brief words on these topics may not come amiss.

a. The presumed misogyny of the Church is the ultimate form taken by prejudices bearing on the celibacy of the clergy and which we have done our best to unmask in their assumptions. *Per se,* this is not an 'argument' worthy of serious consideration except within vulgarizations, as frequent as superficial, of things inherent not only in the priesthood but also in the spiritual life as such. Considering the history of European culture, we are aware of the influence that the first Enlightenment, manufacturer of vulgar libels against Catholicism – forerunners of the media and a degenerate, scandal-mongering press, mean and underhand instruments destructive of the Christian spirit – has had in propagating the most underhand and uncouth forms of anti-clericalism. Were we to consider the course of our recent 'magnificent and progressive destiny', we should know better than to leave the highroad and hence to regress historically. We could also put up a better defence each time the same stale opinions are trotted out, not seldom rekindled by some zealous spirit prone – even if *sub specie democratiae* and making poor use of the democratic criterion – to the ultimate prejudices of 'the age'.

b. One cannot, in fact, avoid observing a certain chronological parallelism between two undeniable historical phenomena: the historical assertion of women's civil rights, and a kind of 'emancipation' of women from situations of 'subjection' for which the Church is mainly held to blame on the grounds that Christian doctrine, with the love and protection of the husband for the wife, demands obedience and respect from the wife for the husband. Now, the question we have to ask is, how can a woman go on respecting and honouring in her husband or in her sons, those 'macho' persons who themselves today too often contribute to the growth of indifference or hostility to religion in their determination to succeed, in their most fatuous and inconsistent worldly curiosity? This is not a woman's job: she is undoubtedly called to 'fulfil herself' as the fashionable for-

173

mula will have it, but no truly satisfying reality corresponds to this *ex parte mundi*.

The Church has offered women the model of Mary, auxiliatrix of the human race since *Mother of the unique High Priest who is Christ*. With this, the Church has not completely 'undergone' the evolutionary process over the exercise of women's civil rights. It has, however, laid down the first condition for them, by recognizing women's supernatural destiny as well as their dignity as persons. Thus, *Christianity alone has freed women from all possible forms of enslavement*, those of a paganism in the past, those of a paganism now returning. The Church, by the words of the popes, has constantly insisted on the positive value it sets on the achievements of women, while exhorting them at the same time not to turn these achievements against their true selves, so as to deny the substance of their femininity. And it has done this with the best of reasons: since the logic of the 'claims' has for the most part been directed by hostility to a 'male-dominated' society – the enemy to be taken on as political, economic, even ecclesial 'power-boss' – rather than by criteria of integration and satisfying growth which would then turn the 'victories' into so many instruments for raising the human race. According to the constant and consistent attitude of the Church, the human race should derive great profit from the rise of the feminine presence in history: not as an 'angel-figure' more or less removed from the harsh realities of the world, as is superficially and commonly objected, but as a forceful character, a decisive and indispensable presence in the destiny of the human race. As to Eve, as to Mary, to women has always fallen an immensely important role in the designs of Providence.

Some deep wrinkles have scarred the face of historical Christianity, since European culture ceased to draw its oxygen from the Christian spirit: evil has been denied, and straightway judgement which recognizes it and distinguishes it from good has been inverted. The true has been denied, and the sceptical face of religious indifference has

174

assumed the mask of a more acquiescent tolerance, an easy and beguiling surrogate for true and demanding love, 'tolerance' artfully preached by intolerance of the truth.

In this climate, which is social, cultural and spiritual all at once, the affirmation of 'feminism' does not include assent – will it do so, or not? that is the crucial question – that the acquisition of the fruitful and Christian exercise of civil rights become what it might have been, that is to say, the affirmation of the positive presence and leading function – the 'constructive' function, that is to say – of the feminine element in the world. For women have never, in such grave mode and measure as today, been the slaves of the less noble powers, that of money and that of the emotions, in the management of which, however, they often demand to share, and indeed do share, whether they know it or not, in the dual role of exploiters and exploited.

It does not seem unfair to say that the other side of this coin of shoddy mintage is paradoxically concealed in the demand for a female priesthood (with husband and children, of course), as though the priesthood *as such* can be interpreted by the same standard as a civil function, the exercise of which is available 'by right'. It is no accident that the pressure is greatest where the theory of the *civil function* of the priesthood is widespread. And this precisely is the state of affairs in a large part of Christendom, and one that is a great worry to the Pastors of the Church.

c. We must, however, be ready to share this worry with them: and make a start with the women. The very acquisition of broader social opportunities and fuller civil rights ought to sharpen a woman's awareness of her *incomparable* influence in the moulding and guiding of the human race: an influence which is harshly tested when the feminine presence elects, by egotistical self-assertion, to negate rather than to build up. In this sense, the influence of woman in the home, the schools, the hospitals, "when negative is humanly irreparable" precisely in proportion to the power of her femininity in the surroundings where she happens to be living and working.

So, to play the part in making the world a better place, all a woman has to do is recognize, within her own family and social surroundings, the equivalent of a priestly vocation (how many 'Christian' mothers are saddened and alienated by the prospect of a priestly vocation *en famille*!) and devote herself lovingly to encouraging this and not put obstacles in the way: let us pray that this basic call not go unheard.

Could this task possibly unfold, attracting and arrogating to itself the affective interest of the priest with all the responsibilities that flow from this? Vis-à-vis the person called to the priesthood, woman discharges a 'maternal' function, co-begetter of vocation itself, with tact and total care, with inner zeal and deep respect. *In this sense, in relation to the priest, woman is 'mother' in imitation of Mary*: the lives of countless priests are strengthened by feminine presences radiant with devotion and generosity. The pastoral function itself uses catecheses entrusted to sensitive, generous minds nourished by charitable, feminine insight: provident, discreet and valuable help for a genuinely charismatic mission. In this way, woman raised by Christianity to be the free and strong 'consort' of an existence destined for immortality, gives the man called to priestly consecration the highest pledge of self by disposing herself towards the fullest and most perfect of spiritual relationships. That one, precisely, which the priest can accept without inner disturbance and also with greatest profit, since it is consonant with the twofold charism linking celibacy to priesthood; not for the 'congruity' of the celibate state (though of course this congruity cannot be denied) but in homage to radical, fruitful, spiritual chastity, which is *a seamless gift of love*, like Christ's garment, prophetic witness to the future life.

d. Likewise, for the priest, in his dealings with the creature to whom he is not bound by the special ties of man to woman (marital ties), other and differing kinds of relationship are possible which are in harmony with the logic of his vocation: these various kinds do not rule out but rather involve the loftiest function of femininity, that of spiritual motherhood: that which, where denied, would also take away natural motherhood's authentic charisma.

There is a supernatural logic which human beings alone can understand – and which is therefore easy to accept – thanks to which the dilemma concealed in the question which has served us as our topic appears in all its spuriousness and inconsistency. The Church is not misogynistic, for the simple and radical reason that celibacy does not, in the last resort, depend on its historical enactments but on that very special congruity to be found at the Christological-ecclesiological level. The higher, total consecration to God does not exclude that love for the female sex which should and must subsist in the priest consecrated to God in ways different from those willed by the sacrament of marriage. But to be with Christ with the maximum generosity and charity requires total participation in his mystery of Blood and glory: not indeed by the *renunciation of something* but by *a more inclusive because more universal gift of love,* an *ascesis* fruitful in good for all creatures, all to be loved because seen in the fiery crucible of an *absolute* love.

NOTES

1. The Church has certainly not missed itschance of a reasoned reply to a question which, among others, has been canvassed with a good deal of fuss: the one about the 'rule' of priestly celibacy. This was clearly and unambiguously confirmed at the eighth ordinary assembly of the 1990 Synod of Bishops and above all by the explicit statement in para. 29 (Prop. XI) of the post-synodal Apostolic Exhortation *Pastores dabo vobis*: "The Synod does not wish to leave any doubts in the mind of anyone regarding the Church's firm will to maintain the law that de-

mands perpetual and freely chosen celibacy for present and future candidates for priestly ordination in the Latin Rite. The Synod would like to see celibacy presented and explained in the fullness of its biblical, theological and spiritual richness, as a precious gift given by God to his Church and as a sign of the kingdom which is not of this world, a sign of God's love for this world and of the undivided love of the priest for God and for God's people, with the result that celibacy is seen as a positive enrichment of the priesthood." For a truly Christian conscience these words require no comment.

The spirituality of priestly celibacy

Divo Barsotti

Theologian

Christian perfection is perfection of charity. Just as faith is sure and peaceful adhesion to the truth and does not involve doubts, so charity is the fruit of the Spirit and in each of even its lowest degrees involves an absolute adhesion to God. There is no charity where God is not loved as supreme good: if you think you can share love for him with love for others, you do not love. The order of charity is that God is to be loved with a total love: with all your heart, with all your soul and with all your strength. And as faith excluding all doubt is a gift from God, so too is that charity a gift from God that excludes all division.

But how is a spiritual journey possible, if right from the start of the journey we are within God? On the other hand, were we not in God, how could we be saved, not having reached perfection of charity? But clearly no spiritual life is possible that does not entail the overcoming of human conditions. How otherwise could we transcend ourselves and all created things, so as to reach God and cling to him in faith and love? Faith is a gift from God, and charity is a gift from God. So we must find which route to take to lead us to spiritual perfection. The Spirit does not operate in our nature as an external force, beyond our powers, but in our own gifts. He moves our powers in such wise that our whole nature becomes God's instrument. If we are in grace, we are already in God, but God requires us to cooperate in his activity, and the way we must cooperate in God's activity is by consenting and being docile to the activity of the Spirit.

God transfers us into himself, but in God we can complete 'our' journey, which can be without end in a God without end. What happens in the spiritual life is rather like what happens in ordinary life. At birth we are already human beings, but what a long way we have to go before we can live like human beings! The progress we make in the spiritual life depends on how docile we are to God's activity. Practising the moral virtues then is only the actual expression of a spiritual life, since the practice of these virtues, which depends on the activity of the Spirit, is as it were transparent, is as it were leavened by love. For the virtues of a Christian are enlivened by charity; if not enlivened by charity, they cannot be called Christian. So it may be said, the virtues are, as it were, a kind of embodiment of love and, as there is no Christian virtue without love, so there is no charity in a Christian without the virtues in which charity lives.

There is a journey in the virtues which bespeaks the soul's progress in docility to the Spirit. In this docility, all human behaviour becomes transformed. So, the spiritual life involves all the virtues. In the moral life of human beings you might find one virtue without another, but in the spiritual life of Christians you cannot have one virtue without all the rest.

In the spiritual life of the priest, there is one virtue which postulates all the others but nonetheless seems particularly significant of his state and mission. To speak of the spirituality of the priesthood is particularly to consider this virtue. It is ecclesiastical celibacy. In the practice of this virtue are we then to recognize the priest's particular route towards his own perfection of charity? It might seem that celibacy was not an expression of love; of itself it seems only to speak of renunciation, and besides celibacy is not essentially linked to priesthood.

The term indeed is not a happy one: 'celibacy' as it stands says something negative, that is to say renunciation of marriage, and could even mean a state of life that excludes love and shuts a man in on himself. Quite the reverse: the celibacy of the priest is not intended to mean something negative: by celibacy, the Church desires the perfect chastity of the priest. Priestly spirituality has its truest expression precisely in perfect chastity, since chastity, in the priest, is the actual expression of his charity.

We have said, one virtue postulates all the others, but in any given state of life there is one particular virtue which seems to express and reveal charity best. Were chastity not enlivened by charity, it would be rejection of love. But by celibacy, contrariwise, the Church manifests the desire for its priests to be holy. Chastity in the priesthood, contrary to being a defence against love, is the charism of perfect love, of a love which, like God's, is prevenient, gratuitous, universal.

For the priest's devotion to his mission is not his response to being loved by the brethren: the priest too, like the Lord, has to love first. If he can name any reason for his love, it is because he is particularly drawn by the wretchedness of those he has to save. True, the unique Saviour of all is Jesus the Son of God, but the salvation he has won for all in point of fact reaches each individual through the priestly service of those whom Christ associates with himself in his mission. The gives his life for the brethren; priestly ordination consecrates him to a service from which henceforth he may never be freed: a service demanding the total gift of self. And to no one *per se* can he refuse his love.

How could the priest live this love, were Jesus not living within him? Priesthood demands and at the same time postulates the most intimate union, indeed a certain unity, with Christ: Christ himself must live within him, and Christ's life is love to the point of sacrifice, love till death. This unity with Christ, for whom there is only one life and only one love, cannot be lived without perfect chastity. Priestly chastity is therefore, as it were, the sacramental sign of the priest's union with Christ.

It has often been said and we say it again: the priest is 'another Christ'. In the exercise of the priesthood, every priest acts in the person of Christ, but that which comes about by the power conferred on him in ordination, though *per se* assuring the efficacity of his sacramental acts, nonetheless demands that the priest's life – lest it be a lie – be one with Christ's.

So, contrary to living the rejection of love, in chastity the priest realizes that nuptial union which, according to the greatest spiritual masters, is indeed the very perfection of spiritual life. Were it not so, chastity could not become a condition of loving, and would instead become a condition of self-centredness, closing the priest's soul and heart, making his life empty and sterile. For marriage was raised by Christ to the dignity of a sacrament because the love of men and women prefigured the union of Christ with the Church. The perfect chastity of the priest is not only a figure of that union, but its more or less perfect fulfilment. Only thus, by becoming one sole Spirit with Christ will the priest live a true participation in Christ's prevenient and gratuitous love and be Christ personified, in him to live his same passion of love, his mission of universal salvation.

Exclusive love for Christ, for whose sake the priest freely renounces having a family of his own, so dilates his heart as to make him capable of a love that knows no bounds. His family is the universe. True, human conditioning persists. Even Jesus was only sent to the lost sheep of the house of Israel, but this did not prevent him from being in fact the Saviour of the world. If on the visible and social plane a limit is set to a man's activity, charity knows no limit other than its own imperfection. This is why the priest too receives a canonical mission limited in time and space, but the charity that inspires him, of itself, knows no bounds, is eternal and cannot exclude anyone.

One and indivisible is the mission of Christ, and each of us Christians lives it in the state of life in which the Lord has placed us and in those conditions of time and place which Providence has assigned for us to live in. But more than the ordinary Christian, the priest, in the chastity uniting him to Christ in an indivisible charity, is committed to living Christ's own mission. Indeed, it is perfect chastity which opens him to universal charity: nothing and no one ties him down and divides him from others. He is one with Christ, to become one with all.

This union is only accomplished in Christ and involves all humanity, all creation, in a manner being assumed by the Word and becoming one sole Christ in him. Thus the Person of the Word, by whom all things were made, becomes the principle of unity for the whole human race and for the whole creation too; but none of this happens without the priesthood. The priesthood is God's instrument for accomplishing this marvellous design. True, this is mainly by means of the sacraments that we priests administer, but more important still by the witness of our whole lives.

We are taught that Holy Order sets a seal on the nature of the priest. Character does not radically transform human nature but makes it so that each activity of this nature cannot be other than a priestly activity. With all his life, the priest is at the service of the Word, to lead human beings and the world back to Him. For this to be done, the physical world must be subjected to the spirit and the spirit to God. Chastity is the force that brings our emotional life back to obeying the spirit; and therefore in chastity lie the first means for freeing us from the slavery of the senses and for ordering us to the spiritual life. The priest should set an example of this liberation in himself, and be our guide. For, as regards chastity, we are all summoned to begin our journey of healing for a human nature fragmented by sin. Hence the importance of chastity in the life of every Christian, but hence the exceptional importance this virtue ought to have in the life of the priest, who is more directly called to live Christ's mission, so that all physical nature too may be ordered to God.

This salvation which is meant to heal the rupture between human beings and God, between human beings among themselves, between human beings and the creation and, lastly, within human beings themselves, which has been brought about by sin, requires that before all else the unity of the human personality be restored. How can the priest be the messenger of and witness to salvation, if he does not by his own life show that he has himself been saved? Once the flesh has been subjected to the spirit, we can then order ourselves Godwards and be safe in God.

But salvation cannot isolate, cannot divide us from our fellow-beings and, for the priestly mission, even less can it divide the priest from all the people to whom he has been sent. Chastity, which heals human nature fragmented by sin, is, in the priest, also a commitment to healing the division sin has caused between human beings, and between human beings and the creation. Perfect chastity is that divine force not only raising human nature up to God but raising the whole creation, by ordering it to him. Important for his sanctification, chastity is supremely important for the priest's ministry. In his freedom from all family ties, he is entirely available for his ministry: nothing can or should divert him from that self-giving to which he was consecrated by priestly ordination. He can no longer lead a life of his own, have a profession of his own, have even a name of his own: he belongs to Christ alone. And in him, Christ lives a mission which the priest can say he has accomplished if Christ asks him for the gift of his whole life. The celibacy the Church wants of him would be a mutilation, were it not, on the contrary, the condition through which the mystery of Christ becomes present in him: the mystery of Christ's life and death for the salvation of the world. To deny there is a sacrifice on the natural plane is to deny the obvious, but the celibacy of the priest is not loneliness if it is union with Christ, nor sterility if it is loving service.

Although it is union with Christ, faithfulness to the pledge of celibacy needs prayer to nourish love, a lively prayer in the priest's personal relationship with Christ. If it is to be loving service, the priest must not shut himself up in himself but feel more and more intensely that he lives for others, that others are his life.

Thus we may sum up the spirituality of the priest: he

ought to live in intimate union with Christ, with him to be one act of praise to the Father and to be together too in serving others. He will live his union with Christ in self-giving to the brethren. Holiness and mission will thus be inseparable and their union will be the fruit of a chaste love. Celibacy, which might seem to isolate him, becomes the sign of a love which, by uniting him to Christ, also makes him a man for all.

Training for priestly celibacy

José Saraiva Martins

Titular Archbishop of Turburnica
Secretary of the Congregation for Catholic Education

The gift of living in fellowship with Christ, following his example, for the glory of God and the service of the brethren in priestly celibacy is a grace and a commitment. For this, there needs to be suitable training. John Paul II's post-synodal Exhortation *Pastores dabo vobis* clearly and precisely affirms the choice of celibacy for candidates to the priesthood in the Latin Church and in some of the Oriental Churches, explains the reasons for it, and gives an account of its values.[1] But it also offers some practical advice for a positive pedagogy of the gift and commitment of celibacy within the framework of training the human personality towards affective maturity.[2] To this effect, the most recent Magisterium of the Church, confirming what has been proposed by previous interventions of the Supreme Pontiffs and of Vatican II, points out the human and spiritual itinerary allowing the celibate life to be lived for "the kingdom of heaven" in the priestly ministry, with a genuine balance between the gift of grace and the radical demands of human love.[3]

The gift of the vocation to celibacy is postulated in the call to the priesthood, without there being any conflict between its radical requirements and its potential realization in its human, bio-psychological and emotional reality. It can and must be lived in humble, serene and positive *moral rectitude* and genuine *spiritual freedom*, freedom allowing the joyous realization of the gift of self in fellowship with the Lord and in his service, for the good of the Church. We are talking here of the celibate life led, with boundless charity, in a human, priestly experience not turned selfishly in on itself, nor gloomily frustrated by lack of emotional equilibrium and absence of supernatural motivation, but permeated through and through with genuine human values, serene in its wealth of feelings, fruitful in works.

Primarily, training for celibacy is a *task that the Church undertakes with regard to candidates for the priesthood*, at the same time that it demands the choice of celibacy and verifies the signs of a genuine divine vocation. For the Church seeks to guide candidates for the priesthood to a full understanding and acceptance of that which is, first of all, the Father's gift to a few (cf Mt 19:11). And it is a task that the Church in its turn entrusts to those appointed to be in charge of priestly training throughout its complex pedagogic itinerary from initial training to refresher courses. This being so, a clear educative line, with definite and positive options, must be at the basis of the undertaking at the various levels of training, from professors of theology to confessors and spiritual directors, from superiors responsible for discernment and vocational training to the very environment in which the training takes place and to the training programmes unyieldingly, with a practical and realistic view of the demands that a real and joyous choice and experience of celibacy makes today in our society, and especially reinforced by the witness of life.

Training for celibacy is also, however, a task that the candidate for the priesthood himself cannot refuse, for he, aware of the gift he has received and of the demands it makes in the light of his own experience and of his relationships with others, but above all in his personal and living relationship with Christ, cannot help but be aware of how important the choice of celibacy is. It is a choice which is rooted, like love itself, in the deepest, most intimate and concrete aspect of his personality and which, therefore, must be lived *pari passu* with his physical, human and psychological evolution, in a harmonious synthesis of spiritual and human values and in consciously verifying his inner motivations and the results he is producing.

So it is clear that the training needed for celibacy as total loving response to Christ and his service, involves on the one hand, the mediation of the Church in her clearly postulated doctrine and in its practical pedagogic application. We are talking here of supplying teaching, pedagogy, discernment, individually tailored and constant help, as the celibate life must be one of constancy and growing fidelity. And on the other hand, it demands in the candidate for the priesthood an especially clear and lucid knowledge of the obligations and renunciations entailed in celibacy, and of the practical potentialities of living it, of the bright path it opens to a full realization of the priestly vocation. It simultaneously requires a sincere awareness of its hardships and a constant verifying of it as an effective and positive experience: verification which, to be genuine, may never be divorced from the theological meeting with the Lord in prayer and from sincere manifestation of conscience and life with confessors, spiritual directors and educators.

The Church's first task in training for celibacy is that of the clear doctrinal exposition of its supernatural values. With this magisterial task, the Church's formative role begins. At this source, anyone who feels called to choose virginity for the sake of the kingdom should draw on the truth and life of God's gift "in the obedience of faith", so as to discover the concrete will of God entrusted to the magisterial mediation of the Church, our Mother and Teacher.

It must be clearly stated that the Church of our day has not fallen short in this task. Diverse, insistent, clear interventions of the Magisterium of the Church in our century have drawn attention to the values and demands of celibacy. Be it sufficient to recall the teachings of Vatican II about it and more especially the authoritative synthesis contained in Paul VI's Encyclical Letter *Sacerdotalis coelibatus* of 24 June 1967, as also the continuous and heartfelt interventions of John Paul II. The Apostolic Exhortation *Pastores dabo vobis*, expressing the desire and conclusions of the 1990 Synod of Bishops, clearly sets out and confirms this task. But the Church has, as it were, willed to make its pedagogic principles even clearer by laying down certain practical guidelines for training which, subsequent to Paul VI's encyclical, were issued by the Congregation for Catholic Education under the title *Educational guidelines for training for priestly celibacy*, dated 11 April 1974. These texts all still retain their value and cannot be commented on at length, much less summarized, in this study. Nonetheless, these texts are basic to training for celibacy, be it for the candidates to the priesthood or for those who train them, in that these texts contain the best and most authoritative summary of the teachings of the Magisterium.

Beside such a wealth of magisterial teaching and pedagogic guidelines, our own task, however, is to offer an interpretative key, a clear and precise choice, to explain one postulate of training, with specific stress on the *spiritual* character of these pedagogic guidelines. I say *spiritual*, not in the sense of excluding other aspects, but as it were in quest of a sapiential synthesis of the training for celibacy, which ought to be integrated with the other contributions.

The postulate comprises some essential and fixed points, five to be precise, which, it seems to me, interlock to form a coherent theory of training: affirmation of the values; exposition of the pedagogic guidelines which embody the values in actual life, the practical personal and responsible acceptance of the grace and of the teaching; the needful objective verification and discernment as to the consistency with which the celibate life is lived and the opening to a road of personalization, growth, equilibrium and interiorization in the priestly life.

Education to supernatural values

The postulate of priestly celibacy on the part of the Church is clear in its requirements: to embrace perfect and perpetual continence for the sake of the kingdom of heaven as recommended by Christ the Lord (cf Mt 19:12). The Church requires the living of the call to the ministerial priesthood in a life of chastity which precludes marriage, with all its prerogatives and demands, and all illicit use of one's sexuality. This radical postulate of evangelical celibacy, which seems to stand in absolute contrast to the innate instinct of human love, is neither impossible nor unnatural, nor is it to the detriment of the true values of the person. God's grace makes its realization possible and human experience itself reveals the possibility of a full realization of the person in this freely and knowingly accepted way of life. Such potentiality for realizing the person in lofty, transcendent values brightens the candidates potential and actual vision.

Un-rhetorically and exactly in the manner required, the Church seems to summarize the *supernatural* values of the choice of celibacy round three basic nuclei, which are in themselves able to give a full orientation to the more radical tendencies of human love and sexuality, integrating as they do ideals, motivations and modes of conduct. I mean those three nuclei put forward by Pius XI and Pius XII in their respective encyclicals on the celibate life, *Ad catholici sacerdotii* and *Sacra virginitas*, summarised in the Decree *Presbyterorum ordinis* of Vatican II, n. 16, and expounded by Paul VI in the encyclical *Sacerdotalis coelibatus*: Christological significance, ecclesiological significance, eschatological significance.[4] It is sufficient however, with a few notes, to recall the overall and practical significance of these values, which have to be postulated, expounded, interiorized and lived in constant faithfulness, so that they become personalized and personalizing as value and motivation, taken in and lived as second nature, in such wise as to bridge the gap between the doctrine stated and life as it is lived.

a. As regards the Christological value of celibacy, we have to stress the actual person of Christ and his example, his life filled with love and self-giving to the Father in chaste love and fully realized humanity. If the reality of Christ's divine nature seems to make his experience as regards virginity unique and unrepeatable, the full truth of his humanity is a stimulus for us to measure our humanity against his, his experience against what we experience, for us to make his feelings ours, for us to desire the fullness of his purity and chaste love for his fellow-beings, his total dedication to doing the Father's work. Christ thus is the supreme and definitive reason for priestly celibacy; he illustrates that it is possible, the basic motivation for living it in the Church and world of today. But this involves the threefold dimension of life in Christ, as does every other aspect of being his follower: living *like him*, in imitation and faithfulness to his word; *with him*, in the fellowship of grace and life with his person; *for him*, in vital motivation of action and faithfulness to a covenantal commitment to his person and his gospel.

In pedagogic terms, the Christological significance of celibacy, as proclamation of newness, grace of fellowship and effective personalization of one's own self-realization in love, is absolutely essential, since it is the first, the last the supernatural reason from which all others flow and to which all others tend. This being so, training for celibacy goes *pari passu* with Christological pedagogy, the discovery of the Lord and Master, the demands inherent in being his disciple and the potentialities of an authentic life in Christ in the intimacy and friendship of discipleship.[5]

b. The *ecclesiological* significance, also derived from the Christological one, operates on a twofold practical level, that is to say, education in human love and supernatural love in the practical form of self-giving. On the one hand, the priest, in relation to Christ, is as it were an expression of the ecclesial community; he represents his bride the Church in faithfulness to the unique bridegroom, a faithfulness that the priest lives in virginity and in the absolute gift of himself. But, as regards the ecclesial community, the priest is also the ikon of Christ the bridegroom, being totally given to serving and loving the brethren. Such 'freedom' in loving makes him particularly suitable for exercising his priestly ministry with all the demands it makes, for he can devote all his human and emotional energies to it: hearing and preaching the word of God, dedication to prayer and the celebration of the sacraments. At the same time, celibacy lived in the integration of his affectivity makes him more free, open-hearted, available, universal, to serve the brethren with fresh and lively energy, frequently repaid by the love of the community and, should he be called, to express the greater love of the gift of his own life, as may be required by the supreme demands of the imitation of Christ, for the sake of the Church.

At the *pedagogic* level, a clear and progressive opening of the future priest's heart to the experience of ecclesial service, to the apostolate understood as the free and open-hearted gift of self, is absolutely necessary, as is also an education in understanding other people, in friendship, in compassion, in the serene experience of his own frailty; for this will make the priest merciful and strong, detached from self and open to all. He who loves Christ "loves all that comes from him", as Vladimir Solovyev so beautifully puts it in *The Legend of Antichrist*.[6] Education to detachment in itself, to universalization and ecclesialization of life, that is to say, to living for the Church, are gradually translated into those attitudes of openness, altruism, open-heartedness, which are signs of a consistent maturation in true love and emotional equilibrium, without which there is no authentic or sound experience of priestly life.[7]

c. The *eschatological* significance of celibacy was indicated by the Lord when he told of the mystery of eternal life (cf Mt 19:10-12; 22:29-30). Of this type, of life we can say that it has its roots in the life of God as origin, and has its crown in glory. By living celibately in this life, the priest shows his shining faith in the divine life from which we come and to which we aspire. At the same time, the witness of celibacy consciously relativizes that which for some people is the unique source of pleasure and self-fulfilment in this life, and invites people to look beyond the ephemeral and illuminates the destiny to which we look forward in hope. Thus celibacy puts God in first place, bears witness to values that never pass away, displays to all the hope of greater things, even relativizes that great sign of human love, I mean marriage, destined to be transfigured in glory.

This postulate of the eschatological value of celibacy, *at the level of training*, also has a necessary motivation and a coherent explanation: I mean a motivation which we may call the intra-eschatological dimension of celibacy in history. For the priest is called with his celibate life to a vital service in the community. He makes God's children sharers in heavenly things on this earth, transmits *everlasting life* by the Word and the sacraments, educates his people in values which do not pass away, in such wise that Christians, thanks to his open-hearted devotedness, already live in the coming kingdom.

Yet maybe today we also sense yet another value of celibacy and virginity, namely its effective *spiritual fruitfulness*. To put our thought in anthropological terms, we may say that it is not enough, absolutely speaking, *to pass on life*, which is the noble and holy task of Christian marriage, but we need *to pass on the meaning of life*, too. In a world where life is held in contempt, or regarded as meaningless or as commonplace without a transcendental dimension, next to parents (they too being called not only to pass on life but to educate as well) stands the priest with his ministry of the word, of sanctification, of charity and service, to illuminate the transcendental meaning of life. Although on account of his celibate choice the priest *does not pass on physical life*, nonetheless, with his open-hearted experience and loving service for all, he *gives meaning to life*, as Christ has done, and in a mysterious continuation of Christ's ministry. In this sense, the eschatological dimension of celibacy becomes a concrete contribution to the humanization of life and to its education, in the truest transcendent sense of the human condition. In fellowship with families and married people, the priest feels himself to be an authentic witness and educator of life and of its absolute meaning, lighting up human history, people's joys and hopes, their sorrows and anxieties.

Practical pedagogic guidelines

A coherent and specific education for celibacy is not exhausted by the authoritative and convincing presentation of its supernatural values in the light of faith as proposed by the Magisterium of the Church. It needs concrete presentation in a series of practical pedagogic guidelines which deal with all the positive and negative aspects that the choosing of chastity for the sake of the kingdom entails. It is therefore significant that Paul VI chose to have his programmatic encyclical on celibacy followed by the document issued by the Sacred Congregation for Catholic Education, which has as its title and content: *Educational guidelines for training for priestly celibacy.* Thus we pass from the values of the guidelines, from the ideal choice of celibacy to a practical pedagogy for living it to the full, for it is a matter of supernatural values having to be concretely lived in the reality of human nature with its demands and problems all in all.

And since it is a question of a choice for which the Church asks but which has to be embraced in full freedom of awareness of its obligations, the guidelines have to respond to certain fundamental requirements. For it must not be a blind choice, but enlightened and aware; not left to a spontaneity ignoring the difficulties, but subjected to an *ascesis* at once severe and positive which avoids the difficulties; not divorced from the fundamental root of the person, which is love, but rather rooted in a capacity for loving, for welcoming and offering friendship; not isolated from the totality of life to the point where celibacy becomes one single obsessive obligation, but made easy by attention to other aspects of life integrating the bio-physical and spiritual equilibrium.

Behold then the need for developing pedagogic guidelines in four directions, which we shall simply list by reference to the *Guidelines* aforementioned.[8]

a. *A wise sex education* is needed, and this should aim at informing candidates for the celibate life about everything that concerns the integral dimensions of the human person. A good mental hygiene which tackles problems realistically and teaches candidates how to live at peace with their own bodies and their own feelings and to respect those of others in accordance with gospel morality, is the best basis for a serene and unobsessive, clear and unmuddled view, made available at the right moment, thus cutting out dubious investigations and information from tainted sources. It is a question of offering a balanced, serene knowledge, all the more necessary since the future priest will have to be furnished with a clear awareness of everything concerning sexuality and marriage, for his ministry. Today this education is all the more urgent in its integrity and with the proper respect and modesty, since society through the mass media offers fragmentary and misleading information and convictions. Often, as we shall see further on, information of this type needs to be checked out in the areas of conscience and spiritual direction.

b. Genuine training for chastity cannot do without a timely *ascetic and spiritual pedagogy* concerning the positive education of the heart and its feelings, of the body and its senses, in relation to oneself and to others. And since sexuality is rooted in the inmost depths of the person and has profound repercussions both externally and internally involving the whole person, a positive *ascesis* has to be applied involving the whole person, and a realistic spiritual pedagogy to educate men, in full freedom and conviction, to reject whatever may harm the equilibrium of chastity in thoughts, images, words and conversations, actions, affec-

195

tions. Yet everything with the needful positive orientation of one who knows how to choose the good and shun evil, of one who is convinced he is to make the choice for an authentic moral good. In this field too, the general pedagogic guidelines have to take practical shape in personalized verification, in overcoming subjectivism, in docility to the prompting of grace and in sincere search for moral truth.

c. In reality, training in celibacy is a *training in true love*, at the same time natural and supernatural, in genuine friendship directed towards Christ and the brethren. The test of celibacy lies in the heart, in real love, just as the imbalance of hedonism is rooted in selfishness. The signs of a clear disposition to live the celibate life are those of a person who is open, cheerful, great-hearted, forgetful of self, obliging. Friendship is a divine and human word. Starting from the initial experiences of human friendship, teacher and pupil should discover and educate that initial capacity for loving, which requires exquisite tact if it is to make progress, through purifications and disappointments, phases of light and shade, towards the person's affective maturation: a true love educated to overcome possessive and selfish tendencies (often also marked by the quest for pleasure) and directed towards a balanced relationship with other people. There is no true friendship without suffering and purification; no authentic friendship in priestly life can be built without supernatural motivation. There can be no education to love without a genuine education and mastery of the feelings. The ability to weave an ample net of relationships and communications is needed excluding no one, a maturation of freedom and of growth in altruism with respect to the freedom and personality of others, an ever clearer education in translating friendship into the giving of service.

The insistence with which the Church's documents dwell on the need for human maturation and affective balance is most marked for these two qualities are the results of this necessary education in loving which will make the priest happy and fulfilled in the celibate life, that is to say, in experiencing a strong, loving friendship with Christ and with the brethren, marked by both natural and supernatural equilibrium.

d. A last and necessary pedagogic guideline requires the *all-inclusiveness and balance of the various aspects of the training* so as to meet all the needs and sectors of personal, community and social life. Such an equilibrium is needed in the approach to initial training for the sake of a harmonious education; but it needs regular checking, and adjustments whenever there is any indication that the celibate life is heading for the rocks. We refer here to the need not to isolate the commitment to chastity from all the other components of personality and life, from individual and community experience, which require a rich and harmonious combination of human and spiritual values. Celibacy, training for it, experience of it, needs the *humus* of all the other aspects that make up the Christian life and the priestly vocation. Chastity is not a gospel flower enclosed within some greenhouse, but growing alongside all the other blooms in the garden of evangelical life. It needs a positive, orderly, clean, outdoor environment; chastity harmonizes with the demands of work and study, grows stronger in the commitment of a genuine personal and community piety, expands in the fellowship of human relations. It needs to be balanced to be healthy, it needs regular times set aside for rest and recreation, the activity of some kind of sport, and some kind of artistic or intellectual hobby; it matures with the initial experiences of apostolate and service to others. The celibate life takes shape and draws strength in the joy of open fellowship, where deeds, words and duties are steeped in truth and cordiality.

Because of all this, the pedagogic guidelines have to be sustained and strengthened by basic, practical, pedagogic decisions in our teaching establishments, in such wise that these do indeed offer the mark and as it were the 'imprint' of a wide range of values and a clear and positive presentation of aspects of life.

A personal response in freedom

Although the authoritative setting forth of the values of celibacy and the relevant pedagogic guidelines is the shining, perennial task of Church and teachers, acceptance above all requires personal commitment on the part of those who are called, so that the celibacy asked for by the Church be a choice made in freedom, assisted by grace. It has, therefore, to be an experience based on truth, and it presupposes a real and practical knowledge of the demands of the celibate life, so as to ingraft a living and real love of celibacy into the substance of the person, each with its own physiology, its own psychology, own impulses, own tendencies, in such a way that there be no dualism, much less any dangerous and false sublimation unable to withstand the shock of difficulties and temptations.

The demands of priestly celibacy are not to be confused with simply not being married, nor indeed with right and proper sexual continence, which gospel morality requires of everyone. The obligations of celibacy are set fair and square in the threefold basic renunciation of sexual activity, of the rich complexity of conjugal love, of the desire for the experience of fatherhood.[9] This threefold tendency, firmly rooted in the person, and which is renounced in the celibate life, should undergo genuine, positive training, without which the person may be damaged, an imbalance be set up in the priest, or a dualism be established between the values which require and make renunciation possible and the actual behaviour of someone who professes the celibate life but in fact does not live it.

But the renunciations also have a positive implication. Clearly the renunciation of licit sexual activity also has its counterpart, at least at the level of gospel choice, in the experiences of the serenity and beauty of chastity itself, of the bliss of purity of heart and body. Not even conjugal love, although an innate tendency, is an absolute, nor is it an indispensable necessity. The celibate life, whether consecrated or not, can express itself in love of service and giving, in friendship, in the richness of human relationships, in intellectual and artistic work, and so forth. Not even fatherhood is an absolute good. The natural tendency to reproduce oneself, with all the beauty of the vocation assigned to our parents by the Creator and Father, can also be discharged in other forms of fatherhood: adoptive, educative, spiritual. The future priest should be able to consider and evaluate these ways in which the human vocation can be fulfilled even outside marriage.

But consecrated celibacy, practically speaking, requires positive training for the threefold renunciation in terms of the supernatural values mentioned above. Educators and those who are preparing for the priesthood should be especially careful to ensure that these supernatural values are accepted and that they cause a real and gradual change of convictions and motivations as well as a redirection towards alternative values, in the practical possibilities offered by the priestly vocation. Three notes seem to be needed about this.

a. Obviously, the threefold renunciation described above does not present itself with the same force and intensity all at once. The sexual problem will always be there, but requires a first and basic training to chastity in adolescence, in youth, so as to lay the foundations for clear consistency between sex education, tendencies and feelings, and behaviour genuinely in accordance with the demands of new life in Christ and of the specific duties and discipleship. The dimension of conjugal love will have its first awakenings in the tendency to relate to the opposite sex, in the initial opening to friendship, to experiencing the attraction that contact with young people can provoke even in the sphere of early experiences in the apostolate. But clearly the problem will recur with other implications in other phases of future priestly life, in private experiences of loneliness, failure and ordeal. This is why a lucid and open, far-sighted and serene education which can give guidance and warning in this field should help the candidates for the priesthood to take stock of these demands arising out of their own nature, so that they can deal with them calmly when the moment comes. The tendency to natural fatherhood and awareness of effectively having renounced it is the last of the tendencies to make itself felt in the celibate priest's heart. But even this will be guided and illuminated as soon as it occurs and be directed towards the realizing of an effective spiritual fatherhood.

b. Plainly the awakening of the three tendencies just described and the effective training for celibate renunciation will have to be undergone in a natural, normal way, with both their positive and their negative aspects, in the inner depths, the sensibility and psychic make-up of the candidates for the priesthood and of the priests themselves. Celibate renunciation is conditioned by positive and negative messages received about it from outside, by the realism with which a sound and truthful training for the life tackles them, or by exaggerated ideas which may arise either because of the culpable silence about these problems on the part of the educators or because of inadequate treatment of the problems and how to solve them, or lastly by the mistaken quest for information, stimuli and opportunities which can disturb the life of priestly celibacy. Although the candidate for the priesthood ought to be aware of his own tendencies and of the most appropriate ways of acquiring adequate knowledge and positive guidance, it is his instructors' job to anticipate, and that is to say meet halfway, in an orderly fashion, the demands for information and positive guidance is such ways as to open up a clear road for a developing awareness of demands, dangers and setbacks in this field.

c. This third comment stems from the conviction that celibacy is a gift of grace. It involves a call and correspondingly an initial enabling by grace to grasp and live its demands in the dynamic of faithfulness appropriate to the vocation and with recourse to the proper means for knowing and living the gift and conditions of celibate life. In the training process therefore, not only is the necessary information to be made available, but the effective capacity to respond, in faith, to the gift is to be stimulated, starting from the initial grace received, by activating all the positive attitudes of faithfulness and openness to the action of the Spirit and by making use of all means leading to practical experience of grace: self-discipline and custody of the senses, training for friendship and work, interior life and prayer, devotion to the Virgin Mary, etc. All, however, in a balance between genuine information and sex education, guidance in the meaning of friendship, human realism in progressively facing problems connected with celibacy and the necessary supernatural dimension of the commitment and of the pedagogy, for a personal acceptance of the gift of grace which celibacy presupposes. There should never be one thing without the other. Otherwise, superficial training can degenerate into a merely human view of sexuality and love, and a spirituality without human basis, coherent pedagogy and perceptive psychology can create false and fragile illusions unable to hold up against the sharp onset of problems and the demands of faithfulness in the midst of temptations.

It is plain, on the other hand, that absence of a specific capacity to grasp and live the demands of the celibate life is the sign of the absence of a specific grace for this: and this leads us to conclude that here we have a candidate who has not received this essential grace, or to discern that there has not been adequate faithfulness to God's 'precious gift' and the charism of the Holy Spirit, which priestly celibacy entails.

Necessary personal and ecclesial verification

Training for the celibate life needs proper and constant verification, in the sense of discernment and of facing up to the truth, as regards this essential sector of priestly life and preparation for it, with its advances and its difficulties, the loss of true motivation or the weakening of fervour, the needful consolidation of gains, the arising of new problems, the necessary vigilance against any kind of presumption even in moments of greatest security. Such checking keeps the doctrinal principles alive and working, inspiring and constantly helping to maintain the ideal, amid the realities of daily life, in constant growth.

There seems to be three ways for verifying and discerning. The more intimate, interior one is concerned with personal answerability to the Lord, who is ever the friend and bridegroom with whom the commitment to celibacy is a real 'covenant' of conjugal love, to which absolute faithfulness is due and for which the Lord promises forgiveness, should it ever be broken by sin. Another is the more exterior, though just as necessary, one of ecclesial verification, of the dialogue with the confessor, accompanied by recourse to the sacrament of Reconciliation with its purifying and fortifying grace, and this accompanied by spiritual direction. This kind of verification overcomes the danger of subjectivism and opens the heart to the search for truth in humility and docility: in the sincere search for truth beyond one's own judgement and one's own opinion, which might sometimes conceal a perilous subjectivism. There is, however, a third way which is not to be ignored and which becomes necessary in many cases: a psychological verification, entrusted to competent persons, whenever candidates evince pathological symptoms that merit expert opinion in the psychiatric field.

a. The first way of verification, the interior one of the relationship with Christ, is undoubtedly the one most needed. It occupies a special place in private prayer, understood as the time of intimacy and truth before God: prayer in which our life and conscience are taken up and laid bare before God, illuminated by the Word: what we really are. Anyone who sincerely wishes to live the celibate life cannot but open his or her conscience before God, with a firm and sincere wish to be illuminated and assisted by grace, with a sincere effort of discernment. In this prayer for self-knowledge and discernment, the candidate for the priesthood should be capable of questioning himself about the true quality of his actions and motivations, about his problems, yieldings and falls if any. In prayer, he should assess the dangers surrounding him and seek remedies which he can and should put into effect so as to keep his oblation to Christ serene and bright in chastity. In special moments of temptation and struggle, this is particularly necessary, while avoiding any sort of dangerous 'repression'.

Only sincere prayer, capable of laying the truth about one's own life before God in one's plea for help, is the kind of prayer that saves, that is to say, that allows the light of truth and grace to penetrate the conscience, that gives one sufficient resolution to amend one's ways and confirms one in a positive course of conversion and renewal. In prayer, interiorization of values takes place, attitudes are judged, guidance is accepted and personalized, important decisions are taken before God, illuminated by the light of his presence, from which nothing is hidden. Prayer is the seat of freedom and true commitment, celebration of the covenant with God, conjugal fellowship with Christ, the search for God's will and, if so be, the beginning of forgiveness and amendment of life.

At the pedagogic level, training for chastity in the celibate life involves training in prayer in this healthy realism of examining one's entire existence before God and of fearlessly allowing oneself to be scrutinized by God and by his love, so as to lay one's problems before him, always, in all truth, and asking for light and strength to overcome them.

b. The other way of verification, as we have said, is that of spiritual dialogue, of sincere and docile openness to one's superiors, to one's spiritual director, to one's confessor, or indeed even to a friend who may help one overcome difficulties and can offer positive guidance for one's life. The danger of subjectivism can even be inherent in prayer, when this does not conduce to the seeking of humble, ecclesial mediation in the form of spiritual direction or sacramental confession. Often the concrete moment of verification, the possibility of a suitable training tailored to one's needs, the chance of dealing with problems in practical terms and of giving precise guidance on celibacy, as opposed to overriding and general principles, lies in this way of spiritual dialogue. If for the one part it is the candidate for the priesthood's own responsibility to seek this encounter to 'get to the truth', it is also the favourable opportunity for educators to exert their practical skills as spiritual guides. Nor should these educators fail in humble boldness to make contact with people, particularly with the young, on the level of actual problems that occur in a training for the celibate life, for two plain reasons:

– Often young candidates for celibacy are like a question not expressed in words but in attitudes, in search of an answer. They show an obvious timidity over tackling a dialogue on this topic; they need a respectful and sensitive initiative to be taken by someone who can reach the heart of the matter and start the dialogue they need and want to set their minds at rest.

– But there is another problem no less important. Today, candidates for the priesthood are drawn from a society which, owing to cultural habits, or ignorance of or contempt for transcendent values, out of growing permissiveness or precocious promiscuity between the sexes, has produced a mentality and often rules of conduct which are unfavourable and often gravely contrary to the requirements of celibate chastity. It is out of the question to suppose that the young men of today come from environments where chastity and virginity are important values at the human level, deliberately inculcated and taught. Indeed, a whole range of permissive habits directly contrary to the demands of chastity and how to preserve it, particularly at certain phases of life, has no importance attached to it at all. There is thus the risk of building on sand, of retaining an erroneous conscience produced by the mentality of the world and which will in the long run have harmful consequences for candidates to the priesthood. It is naive to imagine that candidates already have sufficient training in this respect, and certainly it is not enough just to offer values and guidelines; for verification, there must be personal dialogue as well.

At the formative level, we must encourage cordial openness of conscience, so as to be able to cope properly, with pedagogic realism, with the problems of celibacy. And on the part of those employed in training, this requires clear-sightedness, tact and a great capacity for acceptance and understanding, so as to encourage sincere dialogue on which, as on the rock, to build an authentic system of training for the celibate life.

c. But we cannot overlook a third way of verification which is often needed to integrate the other two and sometimes to clarify the truth about other aspects that do not manage to emerge consciously either through prayer or through spiritual direction. I mean that psychological expertise which in immature persons, marked by traumatic experiences, hereditary tendencies or pathological symptoms, shows itself to be needed, to uncover unconscious negative tendencies, to guide in timely fashion the overcoming of those difficulties, or unequivocally to advise the choice of another state of life, were celibacy to turn out to be exceptionally difficult and in the long run dangerous, either for the young man himself or for the integrity of his priestly life or for the ecclesial community itself.

A journey of growing faithfulness

Training for celibacy, like experience of the spiritual life itself, is a dynamic process, open to the same dimension of priestly existence, to its crises of identity and faithfulness, often connected too with biological and psychological processes, and to its bursts of spirituality and apostolic activity, appropriate to the dynamism of grace and the commitment of a priestly existence orientated towards the holiness of conformation to Christ the Good Shepherd. Two notes on pedagogy are called for.

a. In the light of one approach to training for celibacy, it seems this ought to be concentrated in the period preceding priestly ordination. Obviously a correct education in values, a verification of attitudes, a joyous experience of chaste living, are signs of hope and serene trust which augur a secure future. On the consistency with which the priest can advance in this field depends too the certainty, with the help of grace, of human, spiritual, pastoral and apostolic fulfilment in celibacy – without shadow, even if not without struggle. On the diverse levels of the demands made by the celibate life however, problems arise in acute form in the years following priestly ordination. Today we are well aware of the need for continued training as suitable accompaniment for the discharge of the priestly vocation. Indeed, priestly training, at all its levels, is constantly required for a continual 'rekindling' of the grace of priesthood and the demands of the same.[10]

As regards celibacy, the problem of love and sexuality, the need for balanced and mature relationships with men and women of different ages, the call (which can sometimes be urgent) to effective integration and fatherhood, all come in the years after priestly ordination. Although a positive continuity with previous training is a certain guarantee for the future, this will obviously depend on the priest's actual ability to live in growing faithfulness (as has been mentioned above), as regards values, guidelines and sincere verification in the dialogue of prayer and spiritual direction. The *Guidelines for training* mentioned above, devote a number of important pages to illustrating the difficulties which turn up unexpectedly in adulthood, the reasons for crises in priestly life and the criteria for anticipating and resolving them.[11]

b. The positive and dynamic meaning of celibacy, growth in love for Christ and for serving him, the conjugal gift of oneself to the Church, open-heartedness towards the brethren: all these are innate in the Christian and priestly vocation, which is itself a pilgrimage, a journey, a gradual maturing. The 'trials' and 'hardships', the temptations and crises, are necessary in this, as in any other kind of life. There obviously has to be a purging of the celibate life as it is actually being lived, and this occurs at times when a realistic appraisal is being made of what some renunciations cost at the human level. A further investment of conjugal and pastoral love is required and a consequent renewal of the human and spiritual motivations of the celibate life, lest the impetus decrease and convictions waver, or one should realize that the original motivations are no longer enough to keep one faithful within a dynamic of growth.

The 'crises', as 'trials' of faithfulness imposed by God, are salutary. Purification is a condition normally needed for entering into the full realization of celibacy as total consecration to that love of Christ and the brethren which bears the seal of the paschal mystery: a dying to rise again. Sometimes radical temptations against celibacy work their way in: a wish to catch hold of life, a possible return to a 'normal' human life not deprived of those goods things that celibacy requires should be left behind. It may even seem that the only way out of the crisis, of normalizing one's existence after an experience which at certain moments seems to be self-delusion, would be to go back and start life over again by getting married. This is the supreme moment of trial and crisis, calling for a renewed drive, for a 'new opting for God' in the conviction and joy of self-giving to Christ and the Church.

The fact of the matter is that a final and convinced rootedness in the value of celibacy and in the serene practice of the same, the ability to be a guide and example to others on this road, is often the product of a paschal experience of death and resurrection, of ordeal and victory. However, so as not to become selfishly stuck in a material sort of practice of celibate life without real love, and so as not to grow hardened in a choice one puts up with because there is no going back, the celibate ideal has to be constantly renewed, be its consequences what they may.

This realistic approach absolutely has to be present in any introductory training programme, which must prophetically anticipate what is likely to happen. But it ought also to be present in all the opportunities the Church has to offer in the sphere of on-going training and especially in those high moments of spiritual life which ought to punctuate this continual verification in a dimension of growth in the call to priestly holiness.

Conclusion

Training for priestly celibacy is a synthesis of nature and grace, of ecclesial mediation and personal responsibility, of free choice of giving and of loving concern for the friendship that Christ offers, to be lived in a growing dynamic of faithfulness. As John Paul II says: "Celibacy is to be considered as a special grace, as a gift: 'Not all men can receive this precept, but only those to whom it is given' (Mt 19:11). It is a grace which does not dispense with, but most definitely counts on, a conscious and free response on the part of the receiver. This charism of the Spirit also brings with it the grace for the receiver to remain faithful to it for all his life and to be able, generously and joyfully, to discharge its concomitant commitments."[12] Training collaborates with grace in unity of intention and in docility to the demands of the Holy Spirit, so that celibacy for the sake of the kingdom, the precious pearl of priestly life in the Church, may today too be a shining sign of the presence of Christ, our supreme Model and Master.

NOTES

1. Post-Synodal Apostolic Exhortation of John Paul II *Pastores dabo vobis*, n. 29.
2. *Ibid.*, n. 44.
3. *Ibid.*, n. 50.
4. Cf *Sacerdotalis coelibatus*, nn. 17-34.
5. Cf Decree *Optatam totius*, n. 8.
6. To the emperor's question: "What do you hold dearest in Christianity?" the staretz John replied: "What we hold dearest in Christianity is Christ himself. Him and all that comes from him."
7. Cf *Pastores dabo vobis*, n. 44.
8. Cf also the points set out in the Decree *Optatam totius*, n. 10.
9. Cf *Educational guidelines of training for priestly celibacy*, n. 47.
10. Cf *Pastores dabo vobis*, nn. 70 & 88.
11. *Op. cit.*, nn. 67-69.
12. *Pastores dabo vobis*, n. 50.

Priestly celibacy:
Sign of the charity of Christ

Mother Teresa of Calcutta

We read in the Scriptures how Jesus came to proclaim the Good News that God loves us. He wants us today to be that *love*. Jesus said: "You did it to me": I was hungry, naked, homeless and lonely and you did it to me. I call this – the Gospel on five fingers.

Everyone is called to love God with their whole heart and soul and mind and strength and to love their neighbour out of love for God. But on the night, before he died, Jesus gave us *two great gifts*: the gift of himself in the Eucharist and the gift of the priesthood to continue his living presence in the Eucharist.

Without priests, we have no Jesus.
Without priests, we have no absolution.
Without priests, we cannot receive Holy Communion.

Just as God our Father prepared a worthy dwelling place for his Son in the immaculate womb of a virgin – so it is fitting that a priest prepares himself to take the place of Jesus, the Son of God, by freely choosing priestly celibacy. Marriage and procreation are miracles of God's love by which men and women become his co-workers, to bring new life into the world. But Jesus has clearly spoken to something even greater than that, when he said that in heaven people neither marry nor are given in marriage but live like the angels; and that there are some who have renounced marriage for the sake of the kingdom of God.

Priestly celibacy is that gift which prepares for *life in*

heaven. Jesus calls his priest to be his co-worker in the Church, to fill heaven with God's children.

One day, two young people came to our house and they gave me lots of money to feed the people, because in Calcutta, as you know, we have many many poor people whom we feed daily. And I asked them where they got so much money. They said: "Two days ago we got married. Before marriage we decided that we were not going to buy wedding clothes, we were not to have a wedding feast, but that, instead, we would give you the money to feed the poor." It was something extraordinary for Hindu high-class people to do that. I asked them again: "Why did you do that?" and they said: *'We loved each other so much that we wanted to share the joy of loving with the people you serve."*

To me, this beautiful, living story of two people in love with each other is a *living sign of that oneness of Jesus and his priest.* Here the sacrifice is not money or material things but a higher and better gift – that of priestly celibacy. The greatest gift that one can give to Jesus on the day when one joins the priesthood is *a virgin heart, a virgin body.* We call it priestly celibacy. It is like the virginal love of Christ for his Church, whom the priest represents. The Church is the body of Christ, it is the spouse of Christ.

Celibacy is not only our ability to give but more our ability to accept God's gift, God's choice. Prayerfully reflect how he, the Creator of the universe, has time for you, his little creatures.

Priestly celibacy creates an emptiness to receive that other *wonderful gift* that only Jesus can offer and give – the gift of divine love. First of all, Jesus offers his precious gift of himself for a life-long, faithful and personal friendship with him, in tenderness and love. Nothing will make him give up his faithfulness. He remains faithful.

Dear co-workers of Christ, you have said *'Yes'* to Jesus and he has taken you at your word. The word of God became Jesus, the poor one. Your priestly celibacy is the terrible emptiness you experience. God cannot fill what is full, he can fill only emptiness – deep poverty, and your *'Yes'* is the beginning of being or becoming empty. It is not how much we really 'have' to give, but how empty we are – so that we can receive fully in our life and let him live his life in us. In you, today, he wants to relive his complete submission to his Father. Allow him to do so. It does not matter what you feel, but what he feels in you. Take away your eyes from yourself and rejoice that you have nothing, that you are nothing, that you can do nothing. Give Jesus a big smile, each time your nothingness frightens you. This is the poverty of Jesus. You and I must let him live in us and through us in the world. Cling to Our Lady, for she too, before she could become full of grace, full of Jesus, had to go through that darkness. How could this be done? she asked. But the moment she said *'Yes'* she had need to go in haste to give Jesus to John and his family. Keep giving Jesus to people, not by words, but by your example, by your being in love with Jesus, by radiating his holiness and spreading his fragrance of love everywhere you go. Just keep the joy of Jesus as your strength. Be happy and at peace, accept whatever he gives, and give whatever he takes with a big smile. You belong to him. Tell him, I am yours, and if you cut me to pieces, every single piece will be only all yours. Let Jesus be the victim and the priest in you.

By *freely choosing priestly celibacy* the priest renounces earthly fatherhood and gains a share in the Fatherhood of God. Instead of becoming father to one or more children on earth, he is now able to love everybody in Christ. Yes, Jesus calls his priest to carry his Father's tender love for each and every person. For this reason, people call him 'Father'.

Priestly celibacy is not just not getting married, not to have a family. It is *undivided love of Christ in chastity*. Nothing and nobody will separate me from the love of Christ. It is not simply a list of don'ts, it is love. Freedom to love and to be all things to all people. And for that we need the freedom and poverty and simplicity of life. Jesus could have everything but he chose to have nothing. We too must choose not to have or to use certain luxuries. For the less we have for ourselves, the more of Jesus we can give, and the more we have for ourselves, the less of Jesus we can give. As priests, you must all be able to experience the joy of that freedom, having nothing, having no one, you can then love Christ with undivided love in chastity. That is why, a priest who is completely free to love Christ, the work that he does in obedience is his love for Christ in action. The precious blood is in his hand, the living bread he can break and give to all who are hungry for God.

Let those who are called to follow Jesus in priestly celibacy and to share in his priesthood, pray and ask for the courage to give – 'to give until it hurts'. This giving is true love in action and we can do it only when we are one with Jesus, for in him, with him and through him only, Jesus will be able to do great things, even greater things than he himself did.

There is no comparison with the vocation of the priest. It is like a *replacing* of Jesus at the altar, at the confessional, and in all the other sacraments where he uses his own 'I', like Jesus. How completely the priest must be one with Jesus for Jesus to use him in his place, in his name, to utter his words, do his actions, take away the sins, and make ordinary bread and wine into the Living Bread of his own body and Blood. Only in the silence of his heart can he hear God's word and from the fullness of his heart can he utter these words: "I absolve you" and "This is my body". How pure the mouth of the priest must be and how clean the heart of a priest must be to be able to speak, to utter the words, "This is my body", and to make bread into the living Jesus. How pure must be the hand of the priest, how completely the hand of Jesus must be the hand of the priest, if in it, when the priest raises that hand, is the precious Blood of Jesus. A sinner comes to confession covered with sin, and leaves the confessional, a sinner without sin. O how pure, how sacred a priest must be to lift away sin and to utter the words, "I absolve you."

For me, the priesthood is the sacredness, the holiness for which Christ has come on earth to become man, to live his Father's love and compassion, and to wash away sin. We have a wonderful example of that in the experience with our people.

The sisters found a man and did everything possible for him that love could do for a man who has been shut in like that for years. He did not speak for two days. On the second day, he told the sisters, "You have brought God in my life, bring Father also." So the sisters went and brought a priest and he made his confession after sixty years. The next morning he died.

This is what the priest is – he is the 'connecting link' between humanity and God, just as Jesus was – to take away sin. God had come into this man's life, but that forgiveness for his sin had to come through the priest, to make the connection with God total. This was a miracle of grace that came to that man who had been away from Jesus for so many years, and he expressed it so beautifully: "You have brought God into my life, bring Father also." That connecting, that mercy, that washing away of his sins came through the hands of the priest, and the words of the priest.

The priest has also to *proclaim Christ.* And he cannot proclaim him unless his heart is full of God, and God is love. That is why he needs in the silence of his heart to hear the word of God, for only then, from the fullness of his heart, he can speak the word of God.

You, as God's priest are to be his living instrument, and so you must ever give him permission to do with you exactly as he wills for the glory of the Father. The same spirit will invite you to live an ever closer *oneness with Jesus* – in mind, heart and action – so that all you say and do will be for him, with him and to him. As he is one with the Father, so must you be one with Jesus. As it is with his own priesthood that you have been sealed, so he must be the one to live that priesthood within you. *Nothing and nobody must separate you from Jesus,* so that you can say with St Paul: "It is no longer I who live, but Christ who lives in me."

Christ made himself bread of life to satisfy our hunger for his love, and then he makes himself the hungry one so that we may satisfy his hunger for our love. When St Paul was going to destroy the Christians in Damascus, he was thrown down, and he heard the voice: "Saul, Saul, why dost thou persecute me?" and Paul asked him: "Who art thou, Lord?" Christ did not mention the Christians of Damascus. It is the same thing. "Whatever you do to the least of my brethren, you do it me." If in my name you give a glass of water, you give it to Me. If in my name you receive a child, you receive me. And he has made that a condition also, that at the hour of death we are going to be judged on what we have been and what we have done. He makes himself the hungry one, the naked one, the homeless one, the sick one, the lonely one, the unwanted one, the rejected one, and he says: "I was hungry and you gave me to eat." Not only for bread, I was hungry for love. I was naked, not only for a piece of cloth, but I was naked for that human dignity of a child of God. I was homeless, not only for a home made of bricks, but I was homeless, rejected, unwanted, unloved, a throw-away of society, and you did it to me.

Jesus in the Eucharist made himself bread of life to satisfy our hunger for God, for we have all been created to love and to be loved. And it is very clear what Jesus meant, because how do we love God? Where is God? God is everywhere. How do we love God? And therefore, he gives us the opportunity to do to others what we would like to do to him. To put our love for him in a living action. So, therefore, every priestly vocation is not just to do this or to do that; a priest has been created to belong totally – body, soul, mind, heart, every fibre of his body, every fibre of his soul – to God because he has called him by his name. A priest is very precious to him, a priest is very tenderly loved by God, by Jesus who has chosen him to be his 'second self'. And the work that the priest has been entrusted to do is only a means to put his tender love for God in living action. And therefore, the work that he does is

215

sacred. And the work must always lead not only himself to God, but must be able to lead souls to God. That is why Jesus said: "Let them see your good work and glorify the Father."

You are to be a *radiance of Jesus himself*. Your look must be his, your words his words. The people are not seeking your talents, but God in you. Draw them to God, but never to self. If you are not drawing them to God then you are seeking yourself, and people will love you for yourself, not because you remind them of Jesus. Your desire must be to "give only *Jesus*" in your ministry, rather than self. Remember that it is only your communion with Jesus that brings about communication of Jesus. As Jesus was so united to the Father as to be his splendour and image, so by your union with Jesus, you become his radiance, a transparency of Christ, so that those who have seen you have in some way seen him.

To be able to really be a priest according to the heart of Jesus, you need much prayer and penance. A priest needs to unite his own sacrifice with the sacrifice of Christ, if he really wants to be completely one with Jesus on the altar.

When our Holy Father Paul VI died, I received a trunk call from London asking me what I thought of the death of the Holy Father, and I said: "He was holy, he was a loving father. He had a great love for children and the poor and a special love for the Missionaries of Charity. He has gone home to God and now we can pray to him."

What I said was true of the Holy Father because when he was dying, Mass was being said by his secretary by his bedside. Just at the consecration he suffered the fatal heart attack. Connect this with what he said the year before, when somebody said to him that he was suffering so much, that he was continuing the Passion of Christ, that he suffered more from within the Church because of bishops, priests and religious who were leaving the Church.

Holy Father did not discuss or explain but expressed one short clear sentence: "I am only living my Mass."

By your life woven with the Eucharist, God's love in

Jesus, hidden under the humble appearances of bread and wine, can be lived in all its greatness and beauty in the humble events of daily life. You must continue your Mass after its daily celebration during the Liturgy, by your sincere fidelity to the little moment-to-moment things of life. Like the drops of oil that feed the sanctuary lamp which burns continually near the living Jesus in the tabernacle, your life must continue as a living extension of the Eucharist that you offer. With this Bread you must be broken for many, with this Cup your life must be poured out. Charity is love in action.

Today, many priests are becoming involved in social work and social development, and neglecting the work of their priesthood. But there are many people who can do that. What the people need in a priest is a man who will take tnem to God, who will give them Jesus. They do not need a priest to do social work. There are many good people who can do these things a thousand times better and it is not right for us to take away the work that other people can do so beautifully. No one can do the work of a priest that you are called to do, but only you, as his priest. So, do not *substitute* any other work, however beautiful it may be, for that of your priesthood.

The Missionaries of Charity Fathers – founded in October 1984 – combine the greatness and power of the priesthood with the charisma of the Missionaries of Charity, and so witness to the truth of the Gospel preached to the poor.

I think many, many priests are being called, even without their realizing it, to give themselves totally to the Lord. Yes, the world is in great need of *priests*, of *holy priests*, of *priestly celibacy*, for the world is in need of *Christ*. To doubt the value of one's priesthood and one's priestly celibacy in today's world is to doubt the very value of Christ and his mission – for they are one. Christ's mission is ours.

It is inconceivable how we can turn away from the almighty God and stoop to a creature, however good that creature may be. Is Jesus not the one who can fill you up to the brim with God's love? It is not surprising then, that married people are questioning the Church. In the Catholic Church, there is no divorce. How is it that the Church cannot divorce a married couple and yet a priest can leave his priesthood? A priest may get dispensation but nobody can take away his priesthood. Once a priest, he is a priest forever. In hell also he remains a priest. The Church however, can withhold the use of his priestly power.

Mary, Mother of priests: Contemplate Our Blessed Lady, the Mother of Jesus standing at the foot of the cross of her Son, our only High Priest – with St John the beloved apostle and priest close by her, to whom Jesus said: "Woman, behold your son" and "Son, behold your mother." No one could have been a better priest than the Virgin Mother of God, because she really could without difficulty say: "This is my body... This is my blood" – for it was really and truly her body and blood that she gave to Jesus. And yet she remained only the handmaid of the Lord, so that you and I may always turn to her as our Mother. And she is one of our own, so that we can always claim her, turn to her and be one with her. And of course, that is why she was left behind – to establish the Church, to strengthen the priesthood of the apostles, to be a mother to them, until the Church, the young Church was formed. She was there. For just as she helped Jesus to grow, so she also helped the Church to grow in the beginning. She was left behind for so many years after Jesus ascended to heaven, so that she was the one who helped to form the Church. She is the one who helps to form every priest; and no one can have a greater claim on Our Lady than a priest. And I can imagine she must have had, and she still has, a very tender love and special protection also for every priest, if he only turns to her.

How wonderful then, it is to see that *likeness to Mary*. We *need her*. Let us pray to her that she may obtain for us that great and beautiful gift of priestly celibacy, the sign of the charity of Christ. To this God calls you when he calls you by your name, if he has *chosen* you to be his very own priest, if he has chosen to espouse you with tenderness and love, be not afraid, *follow him.* She will help you, guide you, love you – that you as priests may make the *presence of Jesus even more real in the world of today.*

Put your hand in Mary's hand and ask her to lead you to Jesus. When Jesus came into her life, she went in haste to give him to others. You, as his priest, go with her in haste to give Jesus to others. But remember, you cannot give what you do not have. To be able to give, you need to live that *oneness with Christ,* and he is there in the tabernacle where you put him. Make it a point that first thing in the morning that Jesus be the centre of your life. During the day, learn to pray your work: work with Jesus, work for Jesus. Always keep close to Mary. Ask her to give you her heart so beautiful, so pure, so immaculate, her heart so full of love and humility that you are able to receive Jesus and give Jesus in the bread of life to others. Love Jesus as she loved him and serve him in the distressing disguise of the poor – for we read in the Bible that one of the signs that Jesus was the Saviour to come was that the gospel is preached to the poor.

LIGHT IN THE LORD
Reflections on Priesthood
Cardinal Basil Hume

Light in the Lord is the fruit of a busy life and profound spiritual wisdom and experience. It addresses with compassionate insight the daily life, inner growth, expectations and trials of the priest. The Cardinal's deep love for priesthood shines through on every page.

In *Light in the Lord* Basil Hume, the Benedictine Cardinal Archbishop of Westminster, speaks in the first instance to ordained priests but his message has significance for all who seek a pathway to God through deeper, more authentic inner life.

CARDINAL BASIL HUME OSB, *joined the Benedictine Order at Ampleforth in 1941 and was Abbot of Ampleforth from 1963 until his appointment as Archbishop of Westminster in 1976.*

176 pages   P/B ISBN 085439 399 4   £5.95
                 H/B ISBN 085439 400 1   £7.95

MINISTERS OF YOUR JOY
Reflections on
Priestly Spirituality
by Cardinal Joseph Ratzinger

In *Ministers of Your Joy* Cardinal Ratzinger reflects on
the priestly call, its mission, ministry and response.
The specific theme of these meditations is "priestly
ministry". The aspects which are taken up here are:
witnessing to the Gospel, the meaning of the mission
and the imitation of Christ. Cardinal Ratzinger ana-
lyzes the crisis that has invested the priestly and
religious call and identifies the main cause of it in the
failure on the part of those called to actively witness
in their own life to what the Master had laid down for
them as disciples. These simple and thought-provok-
ing meditations are meant to encourage and strengthen
the desire and decision to follow the Master more
closely in accomplishing the Father's will and in
ministering the Good News to the brethren.

CARDINAL JOSEPH RATZINGER, *born in 1927; profes-*
sor of Theology in the Universities of Bonn,
Münster, Tübingen and Rogensburg; peritus *at*
the   Second Vatican Council; Archbishop of
Munich (1977); from 1981 Prefect of the
Sacred Congregation for the Doctrine of Faith.

128 pages   ISBN   085439 287 4   £5.50